Margaret Bourke-White

Margaret Bourke-White

A PHOTOGRAPHER'S LIFE

Emily Keller

LERNER PUBLICATIONS COMPANY • MINNEAPOLIS

In loving memory of my parents,
Anthony and Jennie Keller

The author would like to acknowledge and sincerely thank the
following people, organizations, and institutions: Dawn Miller, her
editor at Lerner; Carolyn Davis and staff at the George Arents
Research Library for Special Collections at Syracuse University,
Syracuse, New York; the staffs at the Niagara Falls (New York) Public
Library, the Buffalo and Erie County (New York) Library, and the
Lockwood Memorial Library at State University of New York at
Buffalo; the Workshop of the Association of Professional Women
Writers, Niagara Falls, New York; and her niece, Laura McKenna.

Library of Congress Cataloging-in-Publication Data

Keller, Emily.
    Margaret Bourke-White : a photographer's life / Emily Keller.
      p. cm.
    Includes bibliographical references and index.
    Summary: Profiles the life of the photojournalist who was an
original staff photographer for "Life" magazine and a war
correspondent during World War II.
    ISBN 0-8225-4916-6 :
    1. Bourke-White, Margaret, 1904–1971—Juvenile literature.
2. Photographers—United States—Biography—Juvenile literature.
[1. Bourke-White, Margaret, 1904–1971. 2. Photographers.] I. Title.
TR140.B6K45   1996
770'.92—dc20
[B]   92-44382

Manufactured in the United States of America
1 2 3 4 5 6 — JR — 01 00 99 98 97 96

Contents

1   *Growing Up in Bound Brook*   7

2   *Her Father's Daughter*   17

3   *Career Choices*   27

4   *Red Days and Blue Days*   35

5   *A Bright Future*   45

6   *Travel,* Fortune, *and Adventure*   55

7   Life*'s Ace Photographer*   67

8   *War Correspondent*   81

9   *Torpedoes and Bombs*   91

10   *Margaret as Crusader* 101

11   *The Toughest Obstacle* 111

Sources 120

Selected Bibliography 121

Index 122

Heights presented little difficulty for Margaret Bourke-White, but convincing people that she took her own risks to get unique photographs was tougher.

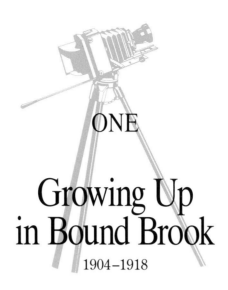

ONE

Growing Up in Bound Brook

1904–1918

Margaret searched for just the right spot to place her camera. Perched on a gargoyle hundreds of feet above the sidewalk, she dared not wiggle much. Shaped like the head of an eagle, the gargoyle protruded from the 61st floor of the Chrysler Building in Manhattan.

Although Margaret was dressed in a cap and warm jacket, she was cold and her fingers were becoming numb. She worked as fast as she could. At 25 Margaret was already a world-famous photographer, and she knew exactly what to do. First, she had to locate the subject of her picture from among the tops of New York's tallest buildings and the ever-changing landscape below her. Then she had to set the exposure, determining the proper shutter speed and aperture (lens opening). Finally, she had to focus the lens from under a dark camera cloth that protected the film from light. Adjusting her camera was never easy, however. Cameras were unwieldy and slow in 1930.

The wind whistled about her. Watching from inside her studio was Oscar Graubner, her assistant. He was setting up his own camera to take a photograph of Margaret.

People sometimes didn't believe that this woman took her own photographs of huge and powerful machines and other factory subjects. Often she climbed high scaffolds, exposed herself to extreme temperatures, and set up her camera in dangerous places to take her photos. A rumor had spread that she was really a man, using a woman's name to get extra publicity. Oscar was taking the picture to prove the rumors were not true.

Margaret took a breath and told herself to relax. She remembered how welders and riveters had taught her about working high above the ground: "Make believe that you are eight feet up and relax, take it easy. The problems are really exactly the same." She soon was absorbed in her view of Manhattan, which stretched below her for miles to the southeast—to the tip of the island and from river to river.

The photograph Oscar took of her that day appeared later in a magazine with the caption, "This Daring Girl Scales Skyscrapers for Art." In the photo, the public saw an example of Margaret's adventurous nature and her dedication to her craft. She would take great risks, if necessary, to get just the picture she wanted.

Margaret Bourke-White had been born in the Bronx, only a short distance from the Hall of Fame. Many U.S. flags had flown that day, June 14, 1904, because it was Flag Day.

Margaret's mother, Minnie White, had been born to English-Irish Protestant parents, and Margaret's father, Joseph White, to Polish Jewish parents. Before their marriage, Minnie and Joseph had left their religions for a faith called Ethical Culture. In keeping with their religious philosophy, the Whites decided to create a mentally stimulating and moral home in which to raise their children. When she was born, Margaret joined her three-year-old sister, Ruth, in the White household. A brother, Roger, was born when Margaret was seven.

Margaret was a toddler when the family moved to Bound Brook, New Jersey. Her father, an engineer and inventor, designed their house for them. Nearby were leafy woods and low hills called the Watchung Mountains.

As a small child, Margaret wasn't afraid of climbing high. But she had other fears: of the dark, of being alone, of bugs. Her parents believed learning to do things without fear was important, so they set out to help her cope with her fears.

One bright, moonlit night, Minnie said something like this to her young daughter: "Let's play a game, Margaret. I'll run this way, you run that way. Let's see who can get around the house faster." Minnie ran quickly so she could catch Margaret in her arms before the child had reached the first corner. Then Minnie laughed. Soon Margaret was running farther and farther in the dark before her mother caught her.

To help Margaret overcome her fears about being home alone at night, her parents would go out for short evening walks. Leaving Margaret with a favorite book of fairy tales or a jigsaw puzzle, they added a few minutes to their trip each night. Before long Margaret didn't mind being alone. She even began to enjoy the solitude. Margaret remembered her mother telling her, "Go right up and look your fears in the face—and then *do* something."

Joseph White helped Margaret get over her fear of bugs and reptiles. He taught her about the life cycles of insects and frogs, and they carefully collected insect eggs to bring home. Sometimes Joseph hid in bushes and whistled bird-calls so real that the bird he was imitating flew over to him.

Margaret cherished the nature walks she and her father took together, often at night. Everything they did together was an adventure.

Margaret was curious about everything—especially snakes. She didn't think they were clammy or too ugly to touch. In fact, she had a pet puff adder. Its neck would swell up, and then it would rise and hiss to try to convince Margaret and Ruth it was a large and poisonous serpent. The children knew it was harmless and would laugh at it. Eventually the snake became completely tame. Often it curled up on Minnie's lap, in a blanket, while she read the newspaper. One day, when Margaret was six, Joseph found a baby boa constrictor in a pet shop and brought it home to Margaret as a pet.

As Margaret was growing up, she was a shy, serious little girl, and she looked older than she was. Even so, she occasionally liked to create some excitement. She knew that a little girl with snakes wound about both her arms would be something no one would soon forget. So one day she took her pet snakes to school. In their fright, the snakes reared up, swelled their necks, and hissed fiercely at the children. Margaret loved the excitement and the attention she got. Because the snakes caused such a panic in the school, however, the principal forbade her from bringing them ever again.

Considering that the love of nature, and especially birds, was what first attracted her parents to one another, it's not surprising that Ruth, Margaret, and Roger would also grow to love nature.

Shortly after learning about snakes, Margaret decided she would become a herpetologist, an expert on reptiles. She often daydreamed about being a scientist, going into the

At an early age, Margaret knew how to get a robin to fly over to her and feed its chick as she held it. Joseph's nature lessons and coaching, no doubt, helped her earn the bird's trust.

jungle and bringing back animals for natural history museums. She told herself she would "do all the things that women never do."

Margaret had several other pets besides the snakes. Some were rabbits and hamsters, and there were two turtles she named Attila and Alaric, who lived under the piano. Her curiosity led her to bring home jellied egg masses and rotting pieces of bark dotted with eggs to see if she could hatch polliwogs, moths, or butterflies.

Once, she fed soft leaves to and tenderly cared for 200 caterpillars under upturned glasses on the dining room windowsill. The whole family sat up one night to watch a butterfly slowly emerge from a chrysalis before their eyes.

Whenever one of her children developed a special interest, Minnie encouraged further study by leaving books on the subject lying around the house. Margaret read more than other children her age, and she could write and speak very well. Her classmates thought she was smart, but different. Unlike them, she liked bugs and snakes. She never spoke slang or played cards, and she didn't know about the latest movies or any comic book characters.

Minnie White forbade her children from participating in many of the activities their classmates enjoyed. She felt comics were bad for her children's developing artistic taste. Also, Minnie didn't allow the children to chew gum, but

Minnie White reads to her children.

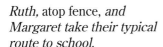
Ruth, atop fence, *and Margaret take their typical route to school.*

Margaret and Ruth would chew gum anyway. So that Minnie wouldn't catch them, they would put their wads of gum on a telegraph pole a block away from home after school. The next morning, the gum would still be there for them to pick up on the way to school.

Margaret had a happy childhood, despite her mother's strict rules. In summer the children tended the garden or went to the beach. In winter they slid down snowbanks. On the frozen Raritan Canal, Margaret and Ruth skated for miles. Skating, plus walks on narrow ledges of fences to and from grade school and the library, improved Margaret's already fine sense of balance and coordination.

Margaret enjoyed snakes so much that she planned to study them in college.

She and Ruth also went to concerts and took music lessons. Margaret loved to perform in dance recitals at school. They were a wonderful release for her great energy. More importantly, dancing satisfied her need to be noticed. She saw the applause as a reward for doing the very best she could. From her earliest childhood days, both her parents taught her to strive for perfection, but Margaret's need to be noticed and rewarded was entirely her own.

Margaret valued the early nature walks with her father, partially because he gave her his full attention then. Inside the house, Joseph was absorbed in thoughts about his inventions, which he was always trying to improve. He worked for Hall Printing Press Company, where he became vice president but forgot to mention it at home.

Margaret's father was a handsome man with black hair and deep-set dark eyes, which often seemed fixed on something in the air when he was in deep thought. Margaret inherited his piercing look, but her blue eyes were fixed on the world around her.

Throughout Margaret's childhood, Joseph loved taking photographs. The walls of their home were full of his pictures. Whatever interested her father was sure to interest Margaret as well. When she was tiny, she would follow him around, imitating him and pretending a little cigar box was a camera. Later, she helped her father develop his prints in the bathtub.

Margaret adored her father. He had answers for her many questions. On Sundays he often took her on trips to factories. Since he loved machines, so did she. He once told her the beauty of machinery was as great as that of nature. The beauty of both, he said, was in their usefulness to humans. Margaret adopted this belief.

Once, he took her to a foundry where workers melted metal and poured it into molds. She climbed up with him on an iron staircase and tried to peer into the dark space around her. Because of the smoke and dust inside the factory, she could hardly see a thing. "Wait," her father said. She felt something special was going to happen.

Soon, high up in the darkness, amid a rush of flying sparks, a gigantic ladle poured liquid fire—molten metal— into casting molds. The molds were for parts to one of her father's printing presses. Margaret was speechless. This was a secret place, and she was certain no other girl her age had seen the wondrous event she was watching.

The power and beauty of that scene, with its fiery colors and huge shapes, stayed in Margaret's memory forever. When she closed her eyes, she could still see it. As she was falling asleep that night, she thought about it and wished she could share it with others.

Roger, Margaret, and Ruth during a family vacation to Niagara Falls

TWO

Her Father's Daughter

1919–1924

Margaret's half-closed eyes opened wide. Miss Gilbert, her English teacher at Plainfield High School, had just announced that this was the last day to hand in themes for a contest. Margaret sat straight up, then turned and looked wildly at Tubby Luf, her best friend. Tubby nodded.

When the bell rang at 3 P.M., signaling the end of the school day, Margaret and Tubby raced to the library. Margaret's composition had to be on the front porch of the principal's home by 5:30.

The theme was to be an 800-word short story. Earlier in her sophomore year, Margaret had signed up for the writing contest only because it would excuse her from taking English exams. After doing nothing on her theme the whole semester, Margaret now realized June had arrived, and with it the final day.

Tubby Luf was a pleasant blonde girl who counted the words as Margaret wrote her story about a boy who wanted a dog. After some time, Margaret polished off the boy-gets-dog section. With five minutes to spare, Margaret and Tubby ran the paper to the principal's house. Later, Margaret learned she had won first prize in the contest, beating out a field of sophomores, juniors, and seniors. For some reason, Margaret believed winning the contest would make boys finally notice her. They might even ask her to a dance.

She had always had plenty of partners for picnics, canoe trips, and barbecues, but never for a dance. Everything else seemed to come her way. She had won honors in English and biology and was an editor for the school paper. Margaret blamed the dark cotton stockings and drab clothes her mother made her wear for her failure to attract dance escorts.

At graduation exercises that year, Margaret collected her prize—three fat green books on moths, frogs, and reptiles. They were tied together with bows of white ribbon. She held them in her arms and waited for the dance that was to follow the graduation ceremony.

As the band began to play, Margaret stood alone, waiting hopefully for a boy to ask her to dance. No boy did. Finally, out of pity, one of her sister's friends came up and asked her to dance. A girl! Margaret wanted to cry. She blinked away her tears of disappointment and put the books down. As the two girls twirled across the floor, Margaret's face was flushed with embarrassment. She wished with all her heart that she could be made invisible.

She didn't talk about her disappointment at home. Earlier that year, Margaret's father had suffered a stroke. Eventually, with a series of daily exercises, he recovered. For a change, he decided to take 18-year-old Ruth, 15-year-old Margaret, and 8-year-old Roger on a trip to Canada.

They traveled through Niagara Falls, and Joseph took pictures while Margaret collected picture postcards. In Canada Joseph wanted to photograph some local children,

Margaret's father, Joseph, at his drawing table

but they froze when they saw his camera. Thinking quickly, Margaret tossed out a coin. As they scrambled for it, her father snapped the scene. Margaret already knew how to get her subjects to act naturally in front of a camera.

After graduation from high school in 1921, Margaret took summer dancing and swimming classes at Rutgers University. In the fall, she enrolled as a freshman at Columbia University in New York. Her life changed greatly, however, when Joseph died after a second stroke in January 1922.

Margaret went back to school soon after her father's death to finish the semester. She studied art and took a course in photography from Clarence H. White, one of a group of highly regarded photographers striving to show photography as an art form. Clarence H. White believed photographs should resemble paintings, and he strove for a misty, soft-focus effect in photography. Margaret imitated his style.

Minnie White was pleased that Margaret was taking up her father's hobby. Even though Joseph White's death had left the family poor, Minnie spent $20 to buy Margaret a secondhand camera with a cracked lens.

In the summer of 1922, Margaret became a nature and photography counselor at Camp Agaming on Lake Bantam in Connecticut. Although the children were often restless and noisy, Margaret could quiet them with stories about nature. She might ask them if they wanted to hear about a real beauty sleep. Then, holding a butterfly chrysalis in her hand, she would delight them with a tale of a caterpillar that woke up to find it had become a beautiful butterfly. She also taught the campers about flowers and snakes, repeating stories and facts her father had told her. The children were awed by her knowledge of wildlife and nature.

Counselors at Camp Agaming arrange stones for a camp activity.

To make a little extra money, Margaret took all kinds of pictures to sell to the campers: sunsets, rolling hills, and campers and their cabins. Even then, she sometimes took great risks for her pictures. One day, at the end of a hike to a mountaintop, she wanted to photograph a view straight down into the valley below. At the edge of the high, steep cliff was a restraining fence. Unafraid, Margaret climbed the fence, set up her big camera, and took her photograph of the breathtaking sight.

In addition to the picture postcards she sold to the campers, Margaret also received orders from townspeople for hundreds more. To coax a couple of the campers into helping with the printing, she would tell them stories and jokes. Margaret had one assistant—another counselor named Madge Jacobson, who had helped Margaret teach photography at the camp. Even though she had help, Margaret often worked alone through the night. She even stayed after others left camp so she could finish printing her postcards. That summer, she printed almost 2,000 pictures. "I am so proud of myself," she wrote in her diary. "I feel as if I could make my living anywhere."

Even so, she hadn't earned enough during the summer to pay her college costs for the next year. With no way to earn or borrow the remaining money, she gave up hope of returning to college. Then she received a surprising phone call from the Mungers, a brother and his sister, in Plainfield. Miss Jessie Munger and her brother had heard about Margaret from a friend and wanted to pay Margaret's college costs for at least a year. They would even buy her a wardrobe so she could enjoy some of the social activities on campus. The Mungers ran an informal scholarship program, sending several young students to college. Joyfully, Margaret

While a student at the University of Michigan, Margaret photographed a horse and rider crossing a bridge.

went off to the University of Michigan in September 1922 to study herpetology.

At the University of Michigan, 18-year-old Margaret discovered stylish clothes. Margaret soon became very popular among the students, where boys far outnumbered girls. However, she had the same interests she had always had. In her dormitory room, she kept a milk snake in her bathtub, and she took pictures for the campus magazine, *The Michiganensian.*

Margaret's pictures were unusual. She frequently managed to include shadows that formed geometric designs. Often the subjects of her photographs were slightly blurred for effect. Although many people complimented her on her photographs, Margaret thought they looked amateurish. Her standards were high.

In spite of her increasing involvement in photography, Margaret continued to plan a career in science. She thought she would give nature lectures to children after she graduated. Her interest in teaching gave way as soon as Alexander G. Ruthven, a noted zoologist at the university, encouraged her to write nature stories for children and to illustrate them with her photographs.

While Margaret was planning ahead for her career, she was totally unprepared for romance, despite her popularity on campus. Then one day at the cafeteria, a good-looking senior engineering student trapped Margaret in a revolving door. He wouldn't release her until she agreed to go on a date with him. He told her his name was Everett Chapman, but everyone called him Chappie. He also enjoyed photography, played drums in a band, and liked to dance. In many ways, he reminded Margaret of her father, especially with his intense concentration in the lab and his devotion to his work. They soon fell madly in love and planned to marry when he graduated in the spring of 1924.

As their relationship deepened, however, something happened to Margaret. Suddenly, she couldn't bear to be alone. She collapsed at mealtimes and woke up at night, sobbing and shaking. At camp in the summer of 1923, she failed to finish a nature study book she had begun writing. When her problems persisted, Margaret made an appointment with a psychiatrist.

Eventually, Margaret revealed to the psychiatrist that she had been hiding a family secret. Sometime after her father had died, she discovered he had been Jewish. Even though she had married a Jew, Minnie White was anti-Semitic. Throughout her lifetime, Minnie made no attempt to hide her dislike for Jews from her children. She hid the fact that Joseph was Jewish from their children until they were grown.

Now Margaret realized that the man she had most loved and admired in her life, her father, and even she herself, belonged to a group of people considered by many to be inferior. She was afraid Chappie might reject her once he knew her background. Margaret was also aware that being Jewish could prevent her from starting a career. In the 1920s, Jews faced discrimination for jobs and were excluded from many social situations. Margaret didn't want her career hampered before it even began.

At the same time, Margaret had other concerns that added to the pressure she felt. Even if Chappie didn't reject her, Margaret was afraid that she might have to forego her plans for a career once they were married. Also, she had an inferiority complex, coupled with conceit—which she readily admitted—and she often felt like an outsider in groups.

Everett Chapman while he was a student at the University of Michigan

After talking over her deepest secrets and fears with the psychiatrist, Margaret felt relieved. She told Chappie that she was half Jewish, and he didn't care. Margaret thought she might be able to combine a career with marriage, and Chappie agreed. They were sure their love for one another would overcome whatever obstacles lay ahead, so they set a date—Friday, June 13, 1924—for their wedding. They weren't superstitious. They thought it would be fun to marry on Friday the 13th.

Then they shopped for a nugget of gold so Chappie could make Margaret's wedding band himself. The night before the wedding, while Chappie was putting on the finishing strokes, the wedding ring broke in two.

Margaret's career soared in Cleveland, Ohio, where she first began taking pictures of industrial sites.

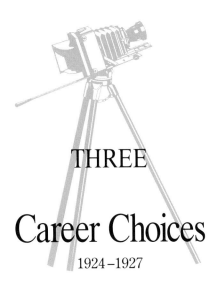

THREE

Career Choices

1924–1927

After their wedding, Margaret and Chappie went to stay in a cottage owned by Chappie's family, on a lake near Ann Arbor. Chappie's mother arrived within days to vacation there, bringing his sister Marian, who was pregnant and had just left her husband. The walls of the crowded cottage were so thin that Margaret and Chappie could scarcely exchange whispers at night without being overheard.

One morning, while Chappie was working at the university, Margaret awoke to the sound of Mrs. Chapman cleaning house. Margaret jumped out of bed to help. While they were working in different rooms, they carried on a conversation. Margaret quickly realized her mother-in-law was angry about the marriage. Before long, Mrs. Chapman was screaming. "You got him away from me. I congratulate you. I never want to see you again."

Completely shaken, Margaret left the cottage and walked 17 miles to the university to find Chappie. When she finally caught up with him, he was little comfort. Over time, Margaret's problems with her mother-in-law persisted, and Chappie couldn't bring himself to confront his mother. Mrs.

Chapman played on Chappie's enormous sense of guilt to control his affections, constantly reminding him of the many sacrifices she had made on his behalf.

In September 1924, three months after their wedding, Margaret thought she might escape her mother-in-law. Chappie took a job teaching at Purdue University in Lafayette, Indiana, far away from Detroit, Michigan, where his parents lived.

Even without the problems Chappie's mother caused, Margaret and Chappie had trouble adjusting to one another and to marriage. Margaret tried hard to please Chappie, but she failed. She cooked nice meals, but Chappie was irritated when she left dirty dishes out. Chappie had always been jealous, possessive, and overly sensitive. Margaret couldn't seem to avoid offending him, and she was troubled by her lack of control over the situation.

Despite the distance between the two cities, Mrs. Chapman still managed to inject herself into Chappie and Margaret's lives. She came on long visits and sent frequent letters. Margaret and Chappie had many bitter arguments, mostly about his mother. After these arguments, Chappie would lock himself in a room. Margaret became desperately unhappy and worried constantly that she was losing her independence. She continued to take classes, enrolling in a paleontology course to study fossils. Margaret also continued making money from her photos, which irritated Chappie. He thought he should provide all their income, especially since he was drawing a good salary.

In 1925 they moved again, this time to Cleveland, where Margaret found a job teaching school children at Cleveland's Museum of Natural History. At night she attended classes in education at Case Western Reserve.

Her mother-in-law thought it was strange that a married woman would remain in college, and she said so often. Most likely, she resented that Chappie paid money for Margaret's tuition rather than contributing it to his parents. After two years of marriage, both Margaret and Chappie realized it wasn't working. Margaret decided to move out.

Her brief marriage to Chappie was the first great failure of Margaret's life. She had exhausted herself trying to make it work, and she left with feelings of rejection and inadequacy. "It was as though everything that could really be hard in my life had been packed into those two short years, and nothing would ever seem so hard again," she wrote in her autobiography.

On her own again, Margaret enrolled at Cornell University in Ithaca, New York. When she arrived in Ithaca in September 1926, Margaret seemed to the other students to be very shy and extremely dedicated to her photography. She didn't go out of her way to make friends, and she revealed very little about herself to those she knew. She never told anyone that she was married.

She chose Cornell not only for its excellent zoology program, but also for the beautiful waterfalls on campus, the ivy-covered buildings, and nearby Cayuga Lake. Before long, she was again taking pictures and selling them as postcards. Margaret still made soft-focused, blurry, artistic pictures.

Margaret's pictures were popular on campus and off. The alumni magazine regularly paid her five dollars for cover photographs. Architects who had attended Cornell wrote to Margaret because they had seen her photographs in the alumni magazine. They told her there were few good architectural photographers in the country and encouraged her to consider a career in the field.

Margaret earned money while attending college by selling prints of campus scenes to students.

Once orders for her pictures began to pour in, Margaret arranged to use the darkroom of Henry R. Head, a commercial photographer in Ithaca, in exchange for a share of her profits. An extra benefit of the arrangement was that Head, working alongside Margaret, gave her enormous technical advice.

Now Margaret faced another dilemma. Should she drop her biology studies to pursue a career in which she had so little formal training? She had a pretty good chance for a job with the Museum of Natural History in New York . . . but to be a professional photographer! She was entranced by the idea.

Margaret wasn't sure how good her photographs actually were, so she sought an unbiased opinion. During her

Easter vacation in 1927, she packed a portfolio and arrived late in the day at the office of New York architect Benjamin Moskowitz. He wasn't expecting her, and when he stepped into the outer office, he was clearly on his way home. Margaret followed him to the elevator. Fortunately for Margaret, the elevator didn't arrive quickly. She had time to bring out her pictures. The photographs stopped Moskowitz.

They returned to his office, and he called in his colleagues. When Margaret left the office an hour later, she did so with the assurance that she could "walk into any architect's office in the country with that portfolio and get work."

Margaret's Cornell pictures sold out during graduation week. On the evening of her graduation, she took the night boat from Buffalo across Lake Erie to return to Cleveland, where she had lived with Chappie. Minnie White also lived in Cleveland, having moved there with Roger four years before. Margaret described the trip across Lake Erie in her autobiography:

> As the skyline took form in the early morning mist,
> I felt I was coming to my promised land: columns of
> masonry gaining height as we drew toward the pier,
> derricks swinging like living creatures—deep inside
> I knew these were my subjects.

In Cleveland Margaret came to love the Flats, a low-lying industrial valley in downtown Cleveland. On the horizon, tall smokestacks stretched high above the steel mills. Office buildings stood on the swampy shores of Lake Erie. Small tugboats pulled huge barges around the Cuyahoga River bend, and coal cars chugged along endless railroad tracks. Traffic darted over arched bridges and blast furnaces puffed billows of smoke into the sky. Margaret thought the Flats were a photographic paradise. She saw movement, rhythmic forms, and dramatic contrasts.

She was especially fascinated with the Terminal Tower, a 28-story skyscraper being built in the center of the Flats. It was the subject of many of her photographs. Margaret hoped her future career in architectural photography would pay enough to allow her to experiment with photographs of the industrial sites she loved. First, she had to find work.

She set up a studio, using her maiden name, but with a hyphen between her middle name (also her mother's maiden name) and her last name. She had started referring to herself this way at Cornell. The name gave Margaret a greater sense of her own identity. She also thought it sounded distinguished as the name of a photography studio.

The more Margaret experimented, the more drama she was able to capture through her lens.

Early in her career, Margaret had a keenly developed sense of professionalism. With her name stamped onto her camera, she looked every bit the professional photographcr.

The Bourke-White Photography Studio opened in Cleveland in the fall of 1927 in Margaret's one-room apartment, which had a pull-down bed in one wall. Margaret set up her stack of developing trays near the kitchen sink. She did her printing in a tiny breakfast alcove and rinsed photos in the bathtub. This makeshift studio was all she could afford.

Photographs like this helped Margaret make an impact in the business world.

FOUR

Red Days and Blue Days

1927–1928

Despite her limited resources, Margaret wanted to make a good impression on her potential clients. She had only one gray suit, but she alternated her accessories—a hat, gloves, and camera cloth—from red one day to blue the next. She kept notes to ensure a client would never see her in the same color scheme on a follow-up visit.

On a "red" day in September, she got her first assignment from some young architects. She was to photograph a new schoolhouse for *Architecture* magazine. Several photos, taken by another photographer, had already been rejected by the magazine's editors.

At the site, Margaret saw litter everywhere: extra lumber, piles of gravel, and leftovers from the work crew's lunches. Mud squished over her shoe tops as she walked around the outside of the building. Despite the mess, Margaret was impressed by the lines of the school. She thought she could get a fine photograph if she waited until sunset, when the bright light would silhouette the building and hide the litter. Unfortunately, Margaret discovered that the sun set on the wrong side of the building.

Sunrise would produce the same effect from the right direction, so Margaret returned to the school before dawn on the next four mornings, only to find cloudy and overcast skies. On the fifth morning, the lighting from the sunrise was exquisite. However, rubbish on the ground obscured the best views.

Undaunted, Margaret cleared away a space, then ran to a nearby florist and bought an armful of asters. She carried them back to the schoolhouse and stuck them into the muddy ground. It worked. Placing herself flat on the soggy ground, she shot her photographs over the tops of the flowers. Then she pulled up her instant garden and moved it to another spot. By the time the flowers drooped, she had shot the school from all angles.

When she delivered the pictures to the architects, they were amazed, especially by the flowers. Soon Margaret was getting assignments from landscape architects who wanted pictures of gardens and estates they had landscaped. The owners of these plush estates also bought her pictures. It was a good source of income, even though Margaret considered the work menial. "I dislike bothering with obvious prettiness," she would say later, "Some architect or decorator has already created it and labeled it beautiful."

Margaret took pictures during the day, then did her darkroom work at night, when she could be sure her kitchen and bathroom were lighttight. One day while making the rounds of potential clients with her portfolio, Margaret saw a preacher in a public square. He was standing on a platform, giving an animated, impassioned sermon. But there was no one in the square to listen to him, except for a flock of pigeons at his feet. Margaret caught her breath. What a picture—but she had no camera with her!

She raced into a nearby camera store and begged to rent or borrow a camera. The middle-aged clerk looked at her curiously through thick glasses, then reached below the counter and handed her a camera. Margaret ran back to the square, pausing only to buy some peanuts. The preacher was still there, but the pigeons were moving away. She tossed the peanuts on the ground to entice them back and then snapped the picture.

When she returned to the store, she found Alfred Hall Bemis, the clerk, eager to help her. They went to lunch to-gether and started to become friends. Something about

When Margaret happened onto this scene, she took quick action to capture it on film.

Margaret's drive and demeanor attracted helpers, people who were always willing to give her a hand. Beme, as Margaret soon began to call him, made a photo enlarger for her from discarded store equipment. At times, when he knew Margaret was too focused on her photography to take time to eat, he took her out for dinner.

Margaret always credited Beme for his impact on her career. He changed Margaret's approach to her work. To guard against technical errors, he persuaded her to shoot several frames of the same shot—and to carry several different types of cameras along so she would have the right one for each situation.

The Cleveland Chamber of Commerce used Margaret's preacher photo on the cover of its monthly magazine. She received $10—a lot of money in 1927—and orders for more photographs to be published on future covers.

With the money she was earning from her commercial photos, Margaret was able to buy supplies to shoot industrial pictures in the Flats. Sometimes she took photographs of bridges, other times of steel mills. She frequently asked at the guardhouse for permission to take her camera inside the steel mills, but she was always turned away.

Margaret sold her first industrial picture to a bank—a partial view of the High Level Bridge. When the bank officer told her to send a bill for $50, Margaret was astonished. That was five times the price she would have asked! Better yet, the bank became a regular client. Each month Margaret brought in a set of industrial pictures, and one was chosen for the cover of *Trade Winds,* the bank's magazine.

Now more financially secure, Margaret bought a used car, which she named Patrick. She also bought material for a new outfit, a purple dress with matching accessories.

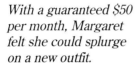

With a guaranteed $50 per month, Margaret felt she could splurge on a new outfit.

One morning, she drove past the Otis Steel mill on her way home and parked the car on a hill overlooking the mill. What she saw made a lasting impression on her. In the early morning haze, coal cars were unloading flaming metal cinders, byproducts of the steel-milling process.

Margaret was awestruck. If the waste from the steel mill could be so spectacular, she had to see what the mill did with the materials it actually used! She wondered if she would ever get inside that magical place.

Margaret continued photographing for architects and landscape artists. She also took and sold her first advertising photograph—of toys for the Higbee Department Store

At first, Margaret relied on advertising photographs and landscape photographs to earn money. At left is the photo of toys done for Higbee Department Store. At right is an example of her landscape photography.

in Cleveland. In December 1927, she showed the photos she had taken of the Terminal Tower during various stages of its construction to the owners, the Van Sweringen brothers. They appointed her official photographer of the Van Sweringen interests. Fully confident in her career now, Margaret set goals for herself. On December 6, 1927, she wrote in her diary: "I want to become famous, and I want to become wealthy."

She met many influential people in her work. Through the president of the Union Trust bank, she was introduced to Elroy Kulas, president of Otis Steel. When Margaret told Kulas her idea of photographing the inside of the steel mill, he was skeptical. He doubted that she would find anything of great beauty in his plant. Plus, another woman who had been allowed inside the mill had fainted from the heat. Even so, Margaret showed Kulas samples of her photography, talked to him about her love for machinery, and assured him she wouldn't faint. Finally, he agreed to let her photograph the steel mill. Kulas gave orders that Margaret was to be allowed inside anytime she came to the plant. Then he left on a lengthy European trip.

Margaret's joy was short-lived. She soon discovered that the steel mills, with their extreme contrasts of light and dark, were very difficult to capture on film. Margaret expected the light from the melted steel to be adequate, but it wasn't. Every picture she took was underexposed. In frustration, she, Beme, and Beme's photofinisher, Earl Leiter, experimented with every type of camera, film, flash powder, and floodlights.

They returned to the steel mill night after night with their equipment. Margaret moved as close as she could to the burning steel, with the mill workers holding up a metal shield to protect her from the heat. The varnish on her camera blistered, and her skin burned slightly, but the pictures still didn't turn out. "I climbed up the hanging ladder into the overhead crane so I could shoot directly down into the molten steel during the pour," Margaret wrote in her autobiography. Even that didn't work.

Margaret's energy and patience were endless, but in February, just when the task seemed impossible, Beme received a visit from a salesman who had some magnesium flares that he hoped to sell to the movie industry. Each flare would give off intense light for 30 seconds.

Over several nights, Beme, Margaret, and the salesman, H. F. "Jack" Jackson, worked like demons. While Jack and

Otis Steel, 1928

Beme held up two flares each, Margaret took three pictures from a crossrail—exposures of eight seconds, four seconds, and two seconds. As the flares remained lit for a few more seconds, she moved in with a hand-held camera to get a couple of extra shots.

When they developed the film, Margaret and Beme were ecstatic. Even sparks flying through the air were visible. Then they discovered another setback. When the pictures were printed, they were dull and lifeless. The photographic paper couldn't reproduce the range of light the film had captured.

In another stroke of good fortune, a salesman named Charlie Bolwell came through town showing samples of a photographic paper containing a richer emulsion that could print a wider range of tones. Not only did the new paper bring Margaret's photographs to life, but Charlie showed Margaret some darkroom techniques to make her prints even better. From him, Margaret learned to appreciate the importance of every step that went into making a good photograph.

Dynamos at the Niagara Falls power plant, 1928

FIVE

A Bright Future
1928–1930

In March Margaret picked the 12 best shots from the mill and went to see Mr. Kulas, who had finally returned from Europe. Her hands sweating, she entered Kulas's office and placed the photos on his desk. He bent over them, examining each carefully. He commented on their originality. Then he asked how much she would charge him for them. Margaret carefully explained that, with the time she had spent and the materials she had used, she would need $100 a picture.

"I don't think that's a lot," he said, "and in any case I am glad to have the chance to encourage you in your pioneer work." He chose eight of the photographs she had brought along, then ordered eight more, all to be used in a book, *The Story of Steel*.

That night Margaret, Beme, and Earl celebrated with a bottle of champagne. It was the first time Margaret had ever tasted champagne.

The industrial pictures created a sensation, making Margaret famous almost overnight. At the same time, *House and Garden* magazine began publishing some of her land-scape photos. Orders began pouring in from industrialists, estate owners, architectural firms, and advertising agencies.

In the spring of 1928, Margaret moved into a studio on the 12th floor of Cleveland's newly completed Terminal Tower. She could afford the rent now, and she needed a real studio because the business had outgrown the small con-fines of her apartment. She also hired a secretary and a technician.

As her career was getting off to a great start, Margaret was quietly closing a chapter of her personal life. In February 1928, Margaret obtained her divorce from Chappie. He was still living in Cleveland, and the two of them had even tried again to salvage their marriage. In the end, they agreed to remain friends.

Margaret frequently took photographs of scenes around Cleveland—and sold several to magazines in the city.

Divorce was viewed by many people as something of a scandal. Margaret was afraid hers would hamper her career, and she was determined nothing would prevent her from being successful. When she gave interviews, she never mentioned Chappie, and she dropped the two years of marriage from her age. Perhaps because she considered her early work amateurish, Margaret also never admitted taking photographs between her freshman course with Clarence White and her senior year at Cornell.

In May of 1928, her picture of Otis Steel's 200-ton ladle won first prize at the Cleveland Museum of Art's photography show. A newspaper headline that month read, "Girl's Photographs of Steel Manufacturing Hailed as New Art." She had arrived in Cleveland just months before, fresh from college, and she was 23 years old. Already she was a success.

In the spring of 1929, Margaret received a telegram that puzzled her:

> Harold Wengler has shown me your photographs. . . . Could you come to New York within a week at our expense? . . .
>> Henry R. Luce, Publisher
>> *Time, The Weekly News Magazine*

Nearly all the photographs *Time* published then were cover shots of politicians. Margaret was not interested in doing political portraits, or any type of portrait for that matter, not when the world of industry was finally open to her.

Margaret's Otis Steel pictures had recently run in several Midwestern newspapers, and she had talked with officials at several industrial firms, including Chrysler Corporation and Republic Steel. She hoped those discussions would lead to steady jobs photographing factories.

Two days passed. Then she picked up the telegram from Luce and reread it. She decided to take Luce up on his offer, since she could use it as an opportunity to call on some New York firms if the meeting at *Time* didn't interest her. Margaret packed her portfolio and soon was in the *Time* office building on 42nd Street near Second Avenue in Manhattan. There she met Henry Luce and Parker Lloyd-Smith.

During their meeting, Luce unveiled plans for a new magazine that captured Margaret's interest. The new magazine would cover only business and industry and would feature the most vivid photographs that could be obtained. Parker Lloyd-Smith was to be the managing editor of this new magazine, which didn't yet have a name. Luce wanted to use Margaret's Otis Steel photographs in a sample magazine that would be shown to potential advertisers. They also wanted her to join the magazine's staff.

Margaret quickly agreed. She was amazed that she should meet these men just at this time—she with her dream of capturing on film the artistic nature of industry and they with their new magazine designed to publish photographs like hers.

Margaret wrote a note to her mother: "I feel as if the world has been opened up and I hold all the keys." Before long, Margaret received a letter from Parker Lloyd-Smith, who wrote that advertisers had loved the dummy magazine. He also told her that the name of the new magazine would be *Fortune*.

With her Cleveland studio taking in all kinds of business, Margaret wasn't ready to move to New York and work full time for the magazine. Instead, she proposed to work half time and was bold enough to ask for $1,000 a month—an astounding amount of money for the times.

Fortune gave Margaret special recognition. One of her Otis Steel pictures had been given a full page in the sample issue, and the caption named her in bold type: "The photographer: Margaret Bourke-White of *Fortune*'s staff now touring the U.S." Under another photograph, the caption read, "Photographer Bourke-White imprisons the glow of molten metal." Photographs taken by others didn't even carry a credit line.

Eight months before publication of the first issue of *Fortune,* the magazine's editors began stockpiling photos and stories that would run in the first issues, so in the summer of 1929, Margaret went on assignment. Her travels brought her to Massachusetts to photograph a shoemaking factory; to Corning, New York, where she photographed one of the last glassblowers to make huge streetlight bulbs by hand; to New Jersey, where she photographed the process of growing orchids from seed to blooming plant; and to South Bend, Indiana, to photograph the businesses in that Midwestern city. Margaret even climbed mountains of fish to photograph a new freezing process. Through it all, photography never failed to thrill her. "I am at the very core a photographer. It is my trade—and my deep joy," she would say.

Margaret's photographs illustrated the cover article, as well as two other articles, for the first issue of *Fortune.* At first, the lead article was to be a piece on International Harvester, a manufacturer of farming equipment. The editors felt it would capture the heart of the American economy and still retain an industrial feel—a perfect article for launching the new magazine. When executives at International Harvester were slow in granting permission for the photographs to be taken, Parker Lloyd-Smith decided

Margaret had taken some photographs—including this one—of the manufacturing steps at International Harvester before Fortune backed away from the story.

instead to feature the hog industry. He accompanied Margaret to Chicago to do the story.

Margaret photographed the pigs through the whole slaughtering process—in the holding pens before slaughter, hanging from hooks on a conveyor belt, being quartered, and so on. One of her best photos was of a line of hogs hanging head down from the conveyor belt. This repetition of form, which she called a pattern picture, became characteristic of her style.

On her last day in the stockyard, Margaret found mountains of hog scraps that would be used to make livestock feed. The stench was disgusting, but Margaret decided she needed the photograph of hog scraps to put the finishing touch on the article. Parker rushed to the car with a hand-kerchief over his nose and shut the windows tight. Margaret stayed behind to get her photographs. Unfortunately for her, the building had very little light, so Margaret had to compensate by leaving her shutter open for long periods—sometimes as long as 15 minutes. When she finally had her pictures, she left her camera cloth and light cords behind to be burned. She knew they could never be cleansed of the awful odor.

Margaret's group of hog pictures was later recognized as one of the earliest photo-essays, casting her as a pioneer in the field of photojournalism. The new format allowed photographs, rather than written text, to impart most of the story.

Between assignments for *Fortune,* Margaret continued to take photographs for clients. In the fall of 1929, she was working on a series of advertising photos for the First National Bank in Boston. She had been spending every spare moment studying a book about football so she could impress a date who was planning to take her to a game. Margaret didn't even take time to glance at the newspapers.

One night Margaret was working late, trying to finish up her photographs of the bank lobby. She thought it would be easier to work through the night, when nobody else would be in the building. To her surprise, bank employees were everywhere—talking excitedly, going into meetings, and rushing around with papers. She became exasperated trying to do her work amid the activity. Finally, a vice president told her why everyone was so agitated: the stock market had crashed.

Margaret was so wrapped up in her photography that she didn't understand the impact of the stock market crash.

Margaret's photograph of the vaults at First National Bank in Boston revealed no sign of the stock market crash that had occurred that day.

People all over the country had lost their fortunes overnight. The crash triggered the Great Depression, a time when banks and businesses failed and millions of people became unemployed and homeless.

During that winter of 1929–30, despite the troubled economy, the founder of Chrysler Corporation wanted to have the world's tallest building bear his name. The publicity value was worth the cost of the building, Walter Chrysler thought. He hired Margaret to photograph the work under construction. She worked on a high, open scaffold 800 feet above the street, photographing a steel tower that swayed back and forth in the freezing wind. At these times, three men would hold down her tripod to keep her camera equipment from falling to the street. When she was done, she had to walk down 50 steps of unfinished stairway inside the building.

In the meantime, the editors and stockholders of *Fortune* worried about launching the new magazine. Potential subscribers had lost their money in the stock market crash. On the other hand, Henry Luce thought even more people would read the magazine because the problems of business were affecting everyone. They decided to go ahead. *Fortune* appeared in February 1930. The big, beautiful magazine cost a dollar an issue in a time when newspapers cost only two cents each. The magazine drew much praise for its brilliant illustrations, Margaret's contribution.

Margaret with an official at the Soviet Embassy

SIX

Travel, *Fortune*, and Adventure

1930–1935

In 1930 Margaret still lived in Cleveland, hosting occasional teas for architects, industrialists, artist friends, and bank presidents in her Terminal Tower studio. Since these were business associates, most were men. Margaret admired men who had power, and they admired her. She dated some of them but made sure she kept her professional life separate from her social life.

She was more of a perfectionist in her work than ever and was determined that her work, and not her friendships, would open doors and earn favors. Even so, she placed a lot of importance on her dealings with these powerful men.

One day, on a visit to New York, she stopped in to see relatives from her father's side of the family, her uncle Lazar and cousin Felicia, who was a social worker. Margaret talked about the influential people she had come to know.

Felicia remarked to Margaret, "Gee, Margaret, it's ironic. You're working for the people who make the people I work for suffer and who command their lives."

Margaret answered sharply, "I'm working for the people that count."

In her specialized, highly paid job, Margaret did not concern herself with the worker who was toiling beside her in the same factory for a few dollars a week. She viewed people mainly as objects for her pictures, using them to show the size of her real subjects—machinery and buildings.

Margaret had proposed the half-time position with *Fortune* for good reason. She had numerous other clients. In the winter of 1929–1930, her photographs began to appear in advertisements that ran in national magazines like *McCall's* and *Ladies Home Journal.*

Advertising work, such as photographing food, was too lucrative for Margaret to give up entirely for a position with an upstart magazine.

In 1930 the Farm Security Administration selected a number of her pictures for an economics textbook. That same year, Margaret's work was included in an exhibit at the Museum of Peaceful Arts in New York. She was so busy that she had to hire six more people to help her in the studio.

That summer *Fortune* sent Margaret abroad to photograph the major German industries. She wanted to go to the newly emerging Union of Soviet Socialist Republics (USSR) as well, where a major change was taking place. The agriculture-based Soviet Union, under Communist leader Joseph Stalin, planned to become heavily industrialized in only five years. In 1930 the Soviet Union was in its third year of a new economic program, and its people had already built many factories. The Soviets were receiving technical assistance from American firms, and the American public was curious about the reforms.

Margaret's colleagues at *Fortune* had little hope that she would come back with photographs, however, since the Soviet government had not allowed any foreign photographers into the country. Still, before leaving the United States, Margaret applied to the Soviet state travel agency for a visa to get into Russia. An official there assured her that her photographs would be her passport. Another commented that her photographs had the "Russian style." With such high praise for her work, Margaret was sure she would be able to pick up her visa at the Soviet embassy in Berlin.

In high spirits, Margaret set off on her *Fortune* assignments in Germany. She photographed nitrogen plants, docks, and a dye works. But when she checked with the Soviet embassy for her visa, she was astonished to learn that no one there had even heard of her. Undaunted,

Margaret continued to press for permission to travel on to the Soviet Union.

After five weeks and several visits to the embassy, she was finally granted her visa. Margaret would be the first foreigner allowed to photograph Soviet industry. She quickly packed her bags, including a trunk full of canned foods (for much of the country was suffering near-famine conditions) and headed to Moscow.

At first Margaret was confined to taking photographs of the factories around Moscow while waiting out yet another round of delays. She had requested permission to travel around the country to take her photographs. Eventually, she was granted freedom to take whatever pictures she pleased. She was also commissioned by the Soviet government to take photographs for several Soviet magazines.

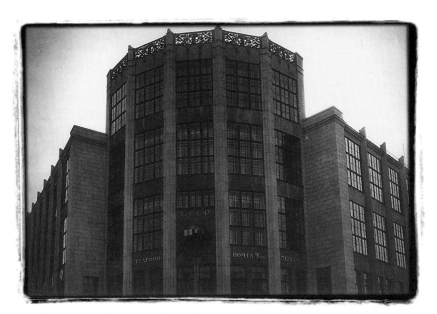

The Post and Telegraph Building in Moscow, 1930

Margaret found that Russians marveled at their new machinery, but didn't know how to use it. At a time when few American women held paying jobs, many Russian women were working in factories, and others were studying medicine and engineering. Margaret noted that the women did so not out of any personal ambition, but because they felt they were helping a common cause—that of implementing their country's huge industrial program.

In Moscow she gave a lecture on photography, and the audience loved her. Some men even made marriage proposals, but her interpreter told them, "Miss Bourke-White loves nothing but her camera."

Back in the United States, Margaret wrote an enthusiastic book about her Soviet experiences, entitled *Eyes on Russia,* which she illustrated with her photographs. The book carried a dedication, "To the memory of my father, who invented machines instead of photographing them." *Fortune* published a portfolio of her Soviet photos in February of 1931.

About two months after she returned from the Soviet Union, Margaret moved from Cleveland to New York. There she would be close to the *Fortune* offices. She also knew she could get more high-paying advertising work in New York. Margaret had been so fascinated with the steel gargoyles of the Chrysler Building that she rented a studio on the 61st floor, from which they extended.

She had her studio designed in the latest fashion—with glass, natural wood, and aluminum. A tropical aquarium was built on a wall, and one of the studio's two terraces was home to a pair of alligators and some turtles.

In the summer of 1931, the Soviet government invited Margaret back for another tour. In less than a year's time, the

On her second trip to the Soviet Union, Margaret photographed a blast furnace under construction in Magnitogorsk.

five-year plan had advanced considerably. This time Margaret took photographs at Magnitogorsk, a giant industrial complex on the site of the richest iron ore deposits in the world. She took a magnificent photo of the world's largest blast furnace under construction there.

Early in 1932, the *New York Times Sunday Magazine* published six articles that Margaret wrote about her second trip to the Soviet Union. In the summer of 1932, she made a third trip, this time to capture the spirit of the people. She planned to travel through the countryside rather than around the industrial sites. She also chose this trip to experiment with motion pictures. Armed with thousands of feet of

In the Soviet Union—yet again—in 1932, Margaret spent more time with people throughout the country.

film and boxes of camera equipment, Margaret made her first stop in Germany.

She stayed in Germany only long enough to photograph German troops training with dummy equipment, such as wooden rifles. At the time, Germany was prohibited from maintaining a large army and stockpiling armaments because of its aggressiveness in World War I. *Fortune* published Margaret's photos of Germany's wooden army with the comment, "It is as yet no threat to the peace of Europe." By showing the training, however, Margaret helped forewarn the public of World War II. Within a few years, Germany would begin an all-out effort to gain control of Europe.

A short time later, in Soviet Georgia, Margaret traveled with the president of Georgia and other officials through the Caucasus Mountains. Because the trip took them far from urban areas and hotels, the group often had to sleep in caves. But Margaret returned with some rare shots. Among the photographs she took were portraits of Soviet leader Joseph Stalin's great-aunt and mother.

During this trip, Margaret exposed 20,000 feet of movie film, donated from Eastman Kodak in exchange for the right to use the film for an educational movie on Russia. To her disappointment, Margaret realized she didn't have a knack for photographing in motion. Her film looked like a series of animated photographs. Even so, Eastman Kodak made its film, and Hollywood cut two short travelogues from her material: "Eyes on Russia" and "Red Republic." None made much of an impact. The project cost Margaret far more money than she made from it. She never used a movie camera again and didn't bother to preserve her films.

Her work in the Soviet Union made Margaret, at age 29, one of the most famous photographers in the United States and won her the respect of intellectuals as well as the general public. She exhibited photographs in museums and lectured on the Soviet Union and on careers for women in photography.

Margaret was sought out for endorsements and did endorse products such as Maxwell House Coffee and Victor records. She always seemed to be in the public eye. She was young, attractive, stylish, well spoken, and much admired.

In 1934, at the age of 30, she was listed in *Who's Who*. Margaret achieved fame, which was one of her goals, but was frequently short of money, even though she was reputed to be one of the most highly paid women in America. A few years earlier, *Time* had written, "Now, at 26, her income is $50,000 a year."

She *did* make a lot of money, especially considering the country was suffering through the Great Depression. But her expenses were high. She had to meet her studio's payroll, buy expensive film and equipment, and pay for travel and studio rent. And there were her extravagances. Stylish clothes were always Margaret's weakness, and she considered them a necessity in her work. As the economy worsened, Margaret had more and more difficulty collecting payments from clients. All she could do was work quickly for as many clients as possible and hope they would pay her.

Before long Margaret was in trouble with her creditors. Rent for the Chrysler Building studio was higher than she could afford to pay, so Margaret often borrowed money— sometimes from her mother, sometimes from friends. In January 1933 she owed back rent on her studio, bill collectors waited in her lobby, other creditors discontinued her accounts with them, and Kodak threatened to stop sending her film. She cut some costs by moving into a less expensive

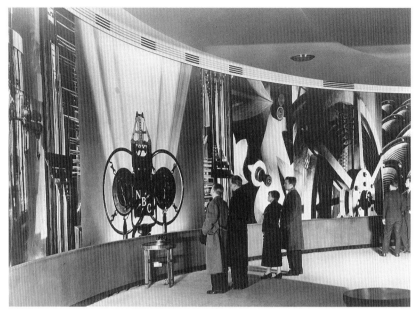

"Trapping the Magical Waves of Sound," Margaret's mural of NBC broadcasting equipment, was on display in the Rockefeller Center for about 20 years.

penthouse apartment and later by sharing her studio with another photographer, who paid half the rent.

Most of Margaret's income came from advertising, and many of her clients insisted she photograph in color. For two years she experimented with color photography, which was in its infancy. The technical process was far more difficult than photographing in black and white, and Margaret eventually lost her patience for it. She looked around for new sources of income and avenues of interest.

Gigantic objects were her specialty and delight, so she jumped at a chance to photograph a mural showing the wonders of radio for NBC. In December 1933, her fascinating series on broadcasting equipment went up in the rotunda at

Rockefeller Center, where it remained until the 1950s. After 1933 she did many other murals.

Margaret was always looking for new frontiers. In 1934 and 1935, Eastern, TWA, and Pan American airlines hired her for aerial photography. These new accounts, plus even more advertising work, helped ease her money problems. A friend lent her a 20-pound aerial camera, helmet, and goggles and taught her how to use the camera. But she had to be strapped into the plane seat because she kept leaning precariously out the door to get a better angle. Margaret loved airplanes and took flying lessons.

In August 1934, one of her editorial assignments was to cover the drought that ran from the Dakotas to Texas. During this assignment, Margaret was struck by the helplessness and despair of the people. She saw children sleeping with damp cloths over their faces so they wouldn't inhale the dust that seeped through cracks in their ramshackle homes. Even though she wasn't able to capture on film the emotion she saw and felt, the images never left her mind.

In 1936, when Margaret was 32 years old, she began an association with Life *magazine that would last the rest of her career.*

SEVEN

Life's Ace Photographer

1936–1939

In July of 1936, Margaret was to photograph a passenger plane flying over New York. She asked people she knew, including her mother, to fill the window spaces.

The day before the flight, Mrs. White—62 years old and still determined to continue her education—registered for summer courses at Columbia University. After registration, she asked to be excused from the following day's class, proudly explaining, "My daughter is going to take me for my first airplane flight." Then she fell to the floor, unconscious. She had suffered a heart attack and died two days later.

Margaret shared her grief only with her family. To cope with her loss, Margaret plunged headlong into her work. Months earlier, she had met the agent for Erskine Caldwell, the author of two popular books, *Tobacco Road* and *God's Little Acre.* She persuaded the agent that she was the one who should accompany the novelist on a trip and photograph conditions of the rural South for his latest project. Caldwell was planning a nonfiction book of pictures and text that would show the poverty and suffering described in his earlier novels. The tall, broad-shouldered author hoped to make the trip during the summer.

Apparently Margaret postponed their trip more than once. She had so much work to finish before she could leave her studio for the several weeks they would travel. Also, there was something exciting developing at *Time* magazine headquarters that spring and summer. *Time,* the magazine that had started *Fortune,* was launching a new weekly picture magazine. This new magazine, to be called *Life,* would tell the news in pictures.

Eventually, Margaret was offered a full-time position on the *Life* staff if she would give up her studio. Not only that, the editors were interested in her collaboration with Caldwell, and they thought they might like to use a portion of the book in the magazine.

When the time came to begin working with Caldwell, Margaret planned to ask for yet another extension—one more week to finalize her other projects and allow her to head into this new venture with a clear mind. She tracked down Erskine by phone in Georgia, where he was more than anxious to get started. Even though he didn't specifically say so, Margaret understood that he wouldn't be working with her; he would do the project without her. Margaret lost no time in settling her affairs and flew quickly to Augusta, Georgia.

Caldwell decided to give her another chance, but he was silent and unfriendly for the first few days of the trip. Margaret didn't understand this gloomy, intellectual man. They traveled in Erskine's car, which was crowded with three people—Erskine, Margaret, and a secretary—and their luggage, Margaret's bulky camera equipment, and two jars of praying mantises that Margaret intended to photograph for the new picture magazine. The three of them traveled through Georgia and Arkansas, with Caldwell stopping to talk to local people and giving Margaret opportunities to take photographs.

On the fifth day, in Little Rock, Arkansas, Caldwell told Margaret he didn't think they were getting anything done, so he wanted to call off the trip. Margaret was stunned. She tried to tell him how much the project meant to her, this opportunity to do something worthwhile. But she couldn't get the words out through her sobbing. Somehow Erskine and Margaret emerged from this episode with a better understanding of one another. The project was back on, and their relationship quickly developed into a romance.

The secretary left a few days later, but by then Margaret and Erskine were working well together. He would engage people in conversation, and Margaret would wait for just the right expression to capture on film.

They traveled through the Deep South, stopping in Georgia, Mississippi, Alabama, South Carolina, Arkansas, and Tennessee. On a dusty road in Georgia, they found a chain gang—a line of prisoners chained together at the ankles to keep them from running away. When Margaret tried to photograph the prisoners, a guard chased them away and fired his rifle at Erskine's car. Later, having acquired an official permit, Margaret got down in a trench and photographed the prisoners in their striped uniforms.

Margaret was awed by what she saw—people so poor they slept on the floor, and sometimes died there. To keep out the weather, people plastered their walls inside and out with newspaper and magazine pages full of ads for items they could never buy. Margaret hoped she wouldn't see an ad for which she had shot a photo.

Everywhere Erskine and Margaret drove, they saw religious signs on the highway. They were welcomed into a black revivalist church, where the passionate sermon incited the parishioners to an emotional frenzy that had them moaning and tossing themselves about on the floor.

There was a lesser-known, almost secret, segment of revivalist churches with all-white congregations. Strangers were unwelcome. Margaret and Erskine sneaked in through a window of one such church in South Carolina as the congregation, in a moment of religious rapture, shouted and waved their Bibles. Women were dancing about wildly, stumbling into Margaret as she was taking pictures. Erskine helped by changing flashbulbs as fast as he could. As the hysteria diminished, Margaret and Erskine clambered back out the window and left town as fast as they could.

A new way of thinking about her photographs was emerging in Margaret. Looking beyond patterns and shapes that she could record on film, Margaret also sought to capture emotion. Later she credited Erskine (by now she was calling him by his nickname, Skinny) with helping her to be more responsive to her subject's personality and moods, rather than injecting her own impressions into the photograph. She hoped, with this collaboration, to launch her reputation as a photographer of social documentary.

Back in New York, the pictorial magazine called *Life* was coming together. There would be four staff photographers on the masthead of the first issue. Margaret was the first named, the only woman, and the only big-camera photographer. She preferred to use big cameras, such as a Linhof, that used film plates for the sharper, more detailed images she could produce. The other staff photographers used the newer, smaller 35-millimeter cameras.

Photographs from You Have Seen Their Faces, *published in 1937*

Margaret's photograph of the Fort Peck Dam was the first cover for Life *magazine.*

Life quickly adopted many of Margaret's standard practices, probably because some of her studio staff followed her there. Margaret brought along her secretary, Peggy Sargent, who was later promoted to picture editor. She also brought along Oscar Graubner, who developed Margaret's film and printed her photographs. One particular practice Margaret demanded was that her prints show a black edge around them—proof that the negative had been printed in its entirety. After fussing over the composition of each scene as she photographed, Margaret wanted to see the whole image on paper, even though she might later crop it to create a better visual impact.

Henry Luce, *Life's* publisher, gave Margaret her first assignment in October: Photograph the construction of Fort Peck Dam. It was to be the world's largest earth-filled dam. The Public Works Administration and the Corps of

Engineers were building it across the Missouri River in Montana to control flooding, produce electricity, and provide irrigation.

Margaret photographed the monumental dam and also the nightlife in boomtowns that sprang up around the construction site. Her photographs so impressed the editors that they selected one of the dam for the magazine's first cover. Many others were used in the lead story—a fully developed photo-essay illustrating American power and technology as a sign of recovery from the Great Depression. Photo-essays were still a new way of presenting information, and Margaret was proud of her role in developing the journalistic form.

The first issue of *Life* was dated November 23, 1936, and copies of the magazine sold out within hours after it hit the newsstands. *Life*'s circulation grew tremendously in the first year, so much that the magazine couldn't keep up with demand. Television hadn't yet been invented in 1936, and *Life* created a common bond among people across the United States.

Some time later, Margaret photographed people in Muncie, Indiana, where federal aid had brought many improvements and helped the city back to economic recovery. Some critics thought it was the best piece of documentary photography that had ever been done, but others believed Margaret was still a better photographer of objects than of people.

When these assignments were complete, Margaret and Erskine finalized their book. Caldwell had written the text, but they wrote the photo captions together. *You Have Seen Their Faces* was published in November 1937. It was featured in *Life* and was a tremendous success, raising public concern and illustrating the environmental and personal damage that poverty had brought to the South.

By this time, Erskine was living in New York. He and Margaret were very much in love, and they saw one another whenever they could.

Margaret wrote articles on the Dust Bowl for *The Nation* magazine and later lectured for a national health care program. Her photographs also appeared in the Museum of Modern Art's "Photography 1839–1937" exhibit, an honor not given to other *Life* photographers.

In July 1937, *Life* editors learned that the governor general of Canada was about to embark on a tour of the Arctic. His journey sounded like a good story, and Margaret was sent on assignment to the Arctic Circle. One

Margaret toured the Arctic and recruited assistants from among her fellow ship passengers to help her photograph butterflies emerging from chrysalides. A chrysalis is just barely visible here, hanging from a stick near the camera lens.

stop was at Fort Norman, where Margaret found a telegram from *Life* asking her also to charter a plane and photograph the Arctic Ocean in the summertime.

The extra assignment turned out to be dangerous. The mail plane she chartered was forced down by mist and fog, stranding the pilot, copilot, Margaret, and two other passengers on a tiny island far from civilization. They had little fuel, few emergency food rations, and a radio signal too weak to call for help. Fortunately, the fog lifted after two days, and they managed to leave.

During Margaret's trip to the Arctic, Erskine sent numerous telegrams urging her to return home so they could marry. These messages distressed Margaret. She couldn't come home, and she was resistant to the idea of being married again.

Even though she loved him, Margaret worried about her relationship with Erskine. If he was upset with her—and she didn't always know why—he might remain strangely silent for days. At other times he would fly into rages, and he occasionally slapped her. She finally talked him into seeing a psychiatrist who had helped her, and she remained firm in her resolve not to marry.

People who knew Margaret at this time spoke of her as a lady, with a touch of glamour. She had poise and used cultured speech. Although distant and self-centered, she had developed charm, thoughtfulness, and good taste. At 33 she was more attractive than ever. In contrast to her young face, her hair was turning white, and she wore the color red to offset it beautifully. She wore little makeup or jewelry, but she had her hair and nails done weekly.

She loved her job at *Life* and would ask for dangerous assignments. She had become a crusader, seeking worthy causes. In early 1938, she set out to cover the corrupt mayor of Jersey City, "Boss" Frank Hague. Hague was pleasant to her but reined in her freedom to work by insisting that she be escorted at all times by the local police, Hague's private army.

Margaret sought to investigate a rumor that Jersey City's slums had a large force of child laborers. One day, she managed to elude her watchful attendants. In a shaky tenement, she photographed a family—including a young child kept home from school to help with the work—that earned $2.50 a day by making paper flowers. She knew the police were close behind her and, after taking the most important pictures, handed her camera to an assistant. He smuggled it out of Jersey City, across the Hudson River to New York. The police burst in on Margaret shortly afterward and rushed her to headquarters. Once there they opened her cameras and ripped out the film, but Margaret was calm. She had outsmarted "Boss" Hague.

Life was also concerned with the growing international fear of a second world war in Europe. The National Socialist German Workers (Nazi) Party, led by Adolf Hitler, had become very strong in Germany. In the spring of 1938, *Life* sent Margaret to Czechoslovakia.

Erskine, who had never been abroad, went with her. Their romance was stronger than ever, and they planned to collaborate on a book about German aggression in Europe and the oppression of Czech minorities. They were in Czechoslovakia several months, but Erskine never warmed up to the Czechs. His silences frightened people into thinking he and Margaret were spies.

On May 28, Hitler threatened to invade Czechoslovakia. Margaret had taken what photos she could, and two days

*During what should normally be a school day for her, a girl helps
the adults in her family make paper flowers. Margaret's
photograph helped substantiate claims that Jersey City's slums
were full of child laborers.*

These two boys are members of Hitler's youth movement, which encouraged them to spy on their families for anti-Nazi activities and trained them in military maneuvers.

later, *Life* printed a 13-page story, combining Margaret's photos with those of John Phillips, another *Life* photographer.

Just before leaving Czechoslovakia in August, Margaret took a photo of trees. They were tall, slender evergreens in a Bohemian forest. She had the picture enlarged to mural size and fitted it on the living room wall of the house she and Erskine had bought in Darien, Connecticut. They had given up their separate apartments in New York to live together.

Their book, *North of the Blue Danube,* came out in April 1939. It was well received, but Margaret felt it was weak because Erskine's behavior had kept them distant from the Czechs. They had intended to portray the bullying tactics of Germans toward minorities, especially Jews, in Czechoslovakia, but the book failed to show this.

Margaret loved Erskine more than any man she had known since Chappie. Despite her misgivings, she finally agreed to marry Erskine. She drew up a marriage contract, stating that he must try to control his moods and not keep her from her work. On February 27, 1939, they flew to Reno, Nevada, to be married. Afterward, they honeymooned in Hawaii.

Some time later, Peggy Sargent, Margaret's secretary, wrote Ruth, Margaret's sister, saying, "Miss Bourke-White seems happier than I've ever known her."

EIGHT

War Correspondent

1939–1942

At first Margaret loved being home and keeping house for Erskine. She had an artist make up a special wallpaper for him, an alphabet in orange, blue, and black letters. For pets they acquired Maine coons, longhaired cats with six or seven toes. Erskine wanted a child and so did Margaret. She and Erskine pretended they had a small child named Patricia. They had dedicated their first book, *You Have Seen Their Faces,* to this imaginary girl.

He wanted her to stay home and write the book on insects she had always planned, and she did finally promise a publisher that she would write such a book. Unfortunately, she never finished it. She was still under contract to *Life,* and she was home only between assignments.

Early in Erskine and Margaret's marriage, war spread across Europe. Hitler's troops invaded Poland on September 1, 1939, and shortly thereafter, Great Britain declared war on Nazi Germany. In October Margaret sailed to England, with plans to continue on to Romania, Turkey, the Middle East, and Italy. *Life* wanted to document Europe preparing for the inevitable war.

In December 1939, Margaret arrived in Romania. As soon as she took out her camera, she was arrested. No one was allowed to photograph alone, and Margaret was forced to work only with an escort of government officials. Finally, she secured permission to photograph without an escort and managed to take pictures of Nazi tank cars loading up with oil, preparing for Germany's attack on Romania.

Working in subzero temperatures, Margaret suffered frostbite on her legs while taking these pictures. She was ordered to bed, and doctors warned her that she might become permanently disabled if she didn't care for her injuries properly. But the next day, she hired a cab and continued taking pictures from its window. By February 1940, her legs were completely healed, and she sailed from Romania to Turkey.

The American public was following Margaret's adventures. In 1940 *U.S. Camera* magazine marveled that a woman was "the most famous on-the-spot photographer the world over." When Margaret arrived in Ankara, Turkey, in February, she found that a freelance photographer hired by *Life* had already been there. She was furious!

For some time, Ralph Ingersoll—former managing editor at *Fortune* and *Life*—had been trying to persuade Erskine and Margaret to join the staff of a publication he was about to launch. He had left *Life* to start a daily newspaper called *PM,* which would devote half its news space to pictures. Erskine was eager for them to work for the new paper.

Margaret made her decision in Syria. She felt that *Life* wasn't printing enough of her photos, nor were they consistent about putting her credit line under the pictures. She decided to go home to work with Erskine at *PM.*

Life managers were astounded by her decision. An editor, Wilson Hicks, received a letter from one of his associates, saying, "There is no doubt at all that she has had a great promotional value and that she has got us into places we couldn't have got into otherwise and also she is a lot better than her jealous fellow photographers will admit."

That she was a better photographer was apparent on the pages of *Life*. Margaret's contributions to the magazine were sharper in line and focus than those of the other photographers, and her photos contained full steps in tone from black to white. Better lighting made objects in her photographs appear sculptured or three-dimensional. Her photos seemed more modern, perhaps because she used the latest techniques and equipment. However, she seldom used the most popular innovation—the 35-millimeter camera. She far preferred the quality of detail she could get only from bulkier cameras, which produced larger negatives.

In March 1940, after returning home from the Near East, Margaret resigned from *Life*. The decision made Erskine happy, because Margaret would no longer be traveling to far-off places for weeks and months at a time. They were still planning to start a family together.

PM regularly showcased Margaret's nature photographs—pictures of eagles, insects, or stages of a rose blooming. Assignments took her to Mexico, into factories, and to Ellis Island. Aside from its dedication to photographs, *PM* brought about several innovations. For the first time, a newspaper listed radio programs, movie show times, and even a crossword puzzle. Critics said *PM* had everything but the news.

On June 14, 1940, the paper ran a story on Germany's invasion of France, but did little more to inform its readers about the war in Europe—the biggest news of the time.

When she joined the staff of PM, *Margaret finally had an outlet for displaying her nature photographs, such as this one of an eagle.*

Margaret soon became disenchanted with *PM,* and four months after she started, she was talking to *Life* about returning to the magazine. Rather than bringing her back to her old staff position, though, *Life* offered her a contract to take assignments for only part of each year.

Her first assignment after she returned to the magazine was to travel across the United States with Erskine. They were to report on conditions in the country—the activity and character of the times. *Life* never used the material, but Erskine and Margaret published it as their third book, *Say, Is This the U.S.A.?* Like *You Have Seen Their Faces,* it depicted the lives of ordinary people, but the photos and text frequently seemed unrelated. Even though the book was praised by reviewers, Margaret recognized its faults.

She and Erskine had another opportunity to travel together in 1941. One of the *Life* editors, Wilson Hicks, strongly believed Germany would invade the Soviet Union that year. Margaret was dispatched to Moscow, and Erskine went along. Many of his books had been published in Russian and were widely read throughout the Soviet Union. Because much of Europe was engaged in war, Margaret and Erskine traveled a safer route through China. They brought with them over 600 pounds of luggage, most of it Margaret's camera equipment.

The trip was long, filled with many delays. Thirty-one days passed between the time they left the United States and the time they arrived in Moscow—and they did all their traveling by airplane! In June, about a month after they arrived, war broke out at the Soviet border. Margaret knew the Nazis

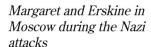

Margaret and Erskine in Moscow during the Nazi attacks

would soon begin attacking the Kremlin, Soviet headquarters in Moscow. She was the only foreign photographer in Moscow—the only correspondent in a position to take photographs of what might prove to be the most important confrontation of the war. However, Soviet officials had announced that their soldiers would shoot anyone spotted with a camera. As usual, Margaret pleaded with the authorities until she was granted an exception. In the meantime, Erskine had agreed to do live radio broadcasts to the United States for CBS, and he had to walk through the streets of Moscow during the bombing raids to get to the studio.

On July 23, Margaret went up to the American embassy roof where the Soviet air wardens couldn't see her. That night she fearlessly photographed bombs as they fell on Moscow. Margaret would later say this was one of the most outstanding nights of her life. The scene from the roof was filled with bright color, glittering light, and a discordant symphony of plane motors, bombs whistling through the air, then the hollow roar as they fell amid the crackle of anti-aircraft guns.

To get her photos, Margaret mounted her cameras on tripods. She focused as well as she could by the light from magnesium flares the Nazis used to reveal their targets, then tripped the shutters to start the exposure, and dashed for shelter as the bombs fell. She hoped that nearby blasts would not shake the cameras and blur her film.

At one point, she sensed that something was heading her way. She grabbed her camera, climbed through a window into the embassy, and lay down against a far wall of the room. A bomb exploded nearby, blowing in every window of the embassy building and pouring glass all over her. A heavy ventilator fell a few feet from her head.

A night raid on Moscow shows the bright glow of parachute flares and the streaks of anti-aircraft fire. Margaret took this photograph from the roof of the American embassy.

Unsteady in her open-toed sandals, she found her way through the building—down stairs and across landings covered with glass—to the basement below. Miraculously, she escaped with only minor cuts. *Life* ran her pictures as a lead story. These were the first photographs Americans saw of the Nazi bombing on Moscow.

All during her stay in the Soviet Union, Margaret tried desperately to photograph Joseph Stalin, the Soviet leader. She had been refused the opportunity on her earlier visits.

Finally, Harry Hopkins, President Franklin D. Roosevelt's personal envoy to the Soviet Union, obtained an audience with Stalin for her. Once inside Stalin's office in the

Kremlin, Margaret was surprised to find that he was short—shorter than her own five feet, five inches—and lean, with pockmarks on his face. He wasn't what the many statues of him had led her to expect. She also found him to be a difficult subject. He refused to show even the slightest bit of emotion as Margaret tried to engage him in conversation. But she finally cracked his steely resolve. Margaret wrote, "As I crawled on my hands and knees from one low camera angle to another, Stalin thought it was funny and started to laugh." She managed to get two photographs of him still smiling. The photographs of the night bombing in Moscow and of Stalin were among the most notable of her career.

As she and Erskine prepared to leave the Soviet Union, Margaret received a cable from her editor, Wilson Hicks. It read, "Welcome Home to the Photographer of the Year." She had proved her reputation all over again. Back home, she

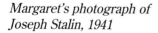

*Margaret's photograph of
Joseph Stalin, 1941*

wrote her own account of the invasion, *Shooting the Russian War,* and went on an extended lecture tour.

Within months after Margaret returned home, the United States entered World War II. In December of 1941, the United States declared war on Japan, in response to the Japanese bombing of Pearl Harbor in Hawaii. Within a week, Japan's allies—Germany and Italy—declared war on the United States.

In the spring of 1942, Margaret requested an assignment overseas. With the United States now involved in battles abroad, *Life* was focused primarily on the war. All war correspondents had to obtain credentials from the War Department. They were assigned to specific military units, wore official uniforms, ate the same food as military personnel, and traveled aboard military planes, ships, or ground vehicles. Margaret served with the Army Air Corps and was the first female photographer to be accredited in the war.

An officer's uniform with an optional skirt was designed for her by the Army War College and became the standard uniform for female correspondents thereafter. She was even given the rank of lieutenant, which would later be upgraded to captain and even later to lieutenant colonel. Margaret was very proud of her uniform and her rank.

Erskine didn't want to go overseas again. Instead, he went to Hollywood and took a job working on a film about the war. He also found a high-paying job for Margaret, but she refused to go to Hollywood. She was at the height of her career, the envy of other photographers, and an inspiration to women everywhere. On November 9, 1942, Erskine cabled Margaret that he had reached the most difficult decision of his life. Their marriage was over. Margaret agreed. All she wanted was the house in Connecticut.

Margaret donned a bombardier suit to take aerial photographs during World War II.

NINE

Torpedoes and Bombs

1942–1946

Margaret was stationed at a secret U.S. air base in England during the summer of 1942. One day a soldier led her to a hangar to show off a B-17 bomber. Her nickname, Peggy, had been painted on one of the engines—a tribute usually reserved only for wives and sweethearts of the crew.

She chose the name "Flying Flitgun" for the plane and broke a bottle of Coca-Cola over its nose during the christening ceremony. A day later, the base's fleet of B-17s took off on its first bombing mission. Margaret was allowed to photograph their departure and then their return after a successful raid on German targets.

Not all of her war photographs were related to combat missions. She also traveled to London for portraits of dignitaries such as Prime Minister Winston Churchill and Emperor Haile Selassie of Ethiopia.

When Margaret first arrived at the air base, correspondents were not allowed to accompany military personnel on combat missions. Eventually the ban was lifted, but Margaret's requests to fly along were always rejected. She wrote about her disappointment in her autobiography: "I

A bomber crewman puts the finishing touches on his crew's tribute to Margaret.

had to go on an actual combat mission. This was the heart and core of it all. . . . The pain of leaving pictures undone which my magazine needed went very deep."

In July Margaret heard the Allies were planning an invasion of North Africa, to start in several months. After much pleading, she was allowed to go along. But she would not be allowed to fly with the initial operation; instead she would travel by the safer sea route. In mid-December, Margaret sailed on the flagship of a large convoy. On board were 6,000 British and American soldiers, nurses, and members of the Women's Army Corps (WACs). The convoy headed straight into the most violent storm the crew members had ever experienced. For five days the storm raged.

Furniture and dishes flew through the air, and people crashed into bulkheads (walls) and each other. The captain insisted on daily lifeboat drills.

During the night of December 22, the flagship was struck by a torpedo. All but one of the other ships in the convoy sped away to avoid any other torpedoes. Margaret first tried to capture the scene on film, but realized the moonlight was too dim for her pictures. In the next instant she knew she must join her fellow passengers in abandoning ship. She wrote in her autobiography that this was her moment of greatest fear. Her mouth went dry. The lifeboat to which she was assigned had been flooded by the torpedo's splash, and there was no rudder for steering. As soon as the vessel was launched, everyone aboard began bailing out water. They rowed quickly away from the sinking ship, but stopped to pick up others—nurses and soldiers on rafts.

Margaret had managed to save one camera, but she wouldn't be able to use it until sunrise. There were so many pictures she wanted to take. The one remaining ship, a navy destroyer, was dropping depth charges all around the sinking flagship to discourage further activity from the enemy submarines. After each drop, the sea ripped open violently. Then the destroyer, too, sailed away. In the dark, ice-cold waters, Margaret's lifeboat drifted away from the others.

Eight hours after the torpedo struck, Margaret's lifeboat was spotted by a British seaplane. Soon a navy destroyer, loaded with hundreds of soldiers rescued from the sinking ship and other lifeboats, picked them up. Before long, *Life* published Margaret's photographs and article of the ordeal, in which she described the incredible courage of the WACs and nurses on board ship, some of whom drowned. Her story made headlines in newspapers across the United

States, and once again, she was the envy of every other news photographer.

The flagship survivors were transported to Algiers, a port city on the northern coast of Africa, where Margaret met with General Jimmy Doolittle. He cleared her to accompany the 97th Bomb Group—her former unit in England—on a combat mission. Margaret would finally have her chance to photograph a bombing raid. The actual mission would be determined by the unit's commanding officer, J. Hampton Atkinson, a tall, handsome pilot from Texas. Although he was married, he and Margaret enjoyed each other's company. In her autobiography, Margaret wrote:

> My most treasured memory of the war is the words of a superb flying officer. I had been planning to take a flight in which there were some elements of risk. Just before the takeoff, he said, "I'm going to fly you myself because if you die, I want to die, too." Nobody died, but I shall carry that short sentence like an invisible star.

At dawn on January 22, 1943, Margaret was in the lead plane, heading for El Aouina airfield at Tunis, a harbor on the Mediterranean Sea. It was used by Germans to ferry troops from Italy to Africa. With the fear of death gripping her, Margaret began photographing as soon as the B-17 was airborne, working as fast as she could before her fingers became stiff. The temperature dipped well below zero as the plane gained altitude.

When they reached the target, the B-17s began dropping bombs, which Margaret saw through her lens as white and black plumes tinged with flashes of red. Margaret's photographs showed fires on the airfield and enemy planes destroyed or severely damaged by Allied bombs. The plane carrying Margaret was struck twice in the wing by enemy fire but was not seriously damaged. *Life* ran the air raid as its lead story: *"Life's* Bourke-White goes Bombing—First Woman to Accompany U.S. Air Force on Combat Mission Photographs Attack on Tunis."

Margaret left North Africa shortly after the combat mission. As she traveled through the United States on a lecture tour, she contacted the families and friends of soldiers she had met to assure them that their men were well.

In September 1943, Margaret returned to the war in Europe. She may or may not have known it, but *Life* had difficulty getting her reaccredited into the military. The Army Air Corps had reported that she had frequently disobeyed regulations in North Africa. Margaret still had admirers in influential places, however, and there was a general who wanted the publicity for his troops that only Margaret Bourke-White could give them. She was allowed to return as long as an army official accompanied her. Margaret was told he was to be her "assistant."

This time she was assigned to the army service forces in Italy. These units were responsible for the crucial task of supplying ammunition and food to troops everywhere. Their numbers also included engineers and the medical corps.

Margaret had survived torpedoes and artillery shells on previous assignments. This time, crawling up hillsides in Italy with the 88th Division, she heard mortar shells whizzing all around her. The enemy fire frightened her even more than the bombs because they were often directed at her rather than at the ship or airplane she happened to be on. She drew on all her courage to return to the front day after day, taking hundreds of pictures. Much of Margaret's time was spent in an area the soldiers called Purple Heart Valley

*Margaret on the
battlefield in Italy, 1943*

—actually Cassino Valley. The terrain of this valley was so rough and the intensity of the battle between the Germans and Allied troops so fierce that both sides suffered heavy casualties. Margaret took her most compelling photographs in a field hospital, where the medical corps treated soldiers wounded in battle, but her package of film was somehow lost after she dispatched it to the Pentagon. She never did find it.

In Italy Margaret met and fell in love with an officer, Jerry Papurt. Jerry had qualities she liked—intelligence, kindness, and a good sense of humor. He also enjoyed dancing. A former psychology professor, he understood the demands of her job and constantly assured her he would never try to keep her from her career. He wanted them to marry.

In the spring of 1944, with her assignment completed, Margaret returned home. She and Jerry wrote to each other every day. She set to work on a book about Cassino Valley, entitled *They Call It Purple Heart Valley*. In it she described the men and women of the army service forces in Italy. One story was about the gallantry she had witnessed at the field hospital and the courage of the surgical nurses there.

In the fall of 1944, the war was coming to an end as Margaret returned to Italy. Allied forces were making huge gains in western Europe and in the South Pacific. While Margaret was at sea, she learned that Jerry Papurt had been captured. Through the Vatican, the Pope's headquarters in Rome, Italy, Margaret sent him the message: "I love you. I will marry you. Maggie." She never knew if he received the message. In November he was killed in an Allied bombing of the town where he was being held prisoner. Margaret immersed herself in recording the "forgotten front," the still fierce battle in Italy.

On April 11, 1945, General George S. Patton's troops marched into Buchenwald, a labor camp outside of Weimar, Germany, with Margaret alongside them. She had gone north to cover the biggest story in the world, the Allied advance into Germany. The Germans were retreating rapidly and had left Buchenwald just hours before Patton's troops arrived. Patton ordered soldiers to gather townspeople to show them what had taken place at the camp. Margaret was one of the first photographers on the scene. She described the day:

> I saw and photographed the piles of naked, lifeless bodies, the human skeletons who would die the next day because they had to wait too long for deliverance, the pieces of tattooed skin for lampshades. Using the camera was almost a relief. It imposed a slight barrier between myself and the horror in front of me.

Hitler's troops had imprisoned millions of "undesirable" people, mostly Jews, in concentration camps throughout Eastern Europe. The vast majority of these people had been put to death—in gas chambers or by electrocution, lethal injection, and execution—shortly after their arrival at the camps. Others had been spared only to provide labor for nearby factories. Until Allied troops began liberating the camps, Germans had denied that such atrocities were taking place. Margaret's photographs helped to prove otherwise.

In addition to showing the horrors of the camps, Margaret sought to document Germany's fall with photos of German cities in ruin. Everywhere she went, there were signs of the German soldiers who had recently left. Finally

Prisoners at Buchenwald had been tortured so often and had seen so much horror by the time U.S. forces arrived that they simply gathered at a fence to await the soldiers who would free them.

After the Allies conquered Germany, Margaret posed with officers on a staircase in the mansion of German munitions manufacturer Alfried Krupp. Margaret had managed to interview Krupp, and notes from her interview were later read aloud during the Nuremberg Trials, in which Krupp was convicted for war crimes.

on May 7, 1945, the Nazis surrendered. The war in Europe was over.

On Margaret's return to the United States, she wrote a book about her German experiences, *Dear Fatherland, Rest Quietly.* It contains many haunting photographs and reveals her hatred of dictators. She pleaded with her country to strengthen its role as a moral leader in the world—by teaching young people in Germany and Italy democratic principles of government.

An Indian girl wears a necklace of English coins—her life savings—around her neck. At the time Margaret visited India, the people's distrust of banks contributed to the country's poverty.

TEN

Margaret as Crusader

1946–1950

Before World War II, Great Britain was the most powerful country in the world, mostly because of its far-flung colonial empire. Lands under British rule or protection included many that were rich in resources.

In March of 1946, Great Britain was losing its hold on the country people referred to as the British crown jewel. India was seeking its independence. *Life* sent Margaret to photograph India's spiritual leader, Mahatma (meaning "Great Soul") Mohandas Gandhi.

When Margaret arrived at Gandhi's camp in Poona, she was impatient to photograph the Mahatma, but his secretary insisted she must be able to use a spinning wheel before she could enter Gandhi's presence.

The spinning wheel was symbolic of Gandhi's drive for freedom from British rule. British law prohibited Indians from making their own goods. Instead, they were to sell their raw cotton to Great Britain and then buy back the cloth manufactured from this fiber. Gandhi urged Indians to spin their own thread and weave their own cloth to keep Britain from profiting.

After a quick lesson, Margaret learned to spin well enough to please the secretary, but she was grateful she wouldn't have to demonstrate her spinning to Gandhi. Next, the secretary warned her that it was Mahatma's day of silence, so she must not speak to him. Nor could she use artificial light while photographing him.

After much pleading, Margaret was allowed to use three peanut flashbulbs. When she entered the hut, Mohandas Gandhi was seated cross-legged on the floor beside his symbolic spinning wheel, reading newspaper clippings. Margaret's photograph of him is world famous. Backlighting makes Gandhi appear saintly.

Margaret photographed Gandhi several times after that session. She traveled with him across India on a train packed with a herd of goats, for Gandhi would not drink cow's milk. (Cows are considered sacred by Hindus.) Gandhi frequently gave prayer talks, and the people adored him; he was winning the battle for a peaceful overthrow of British rule. His goal was a united India.

One person stood in his way. Margaret photographed Muslim leader Mohammed Ali Jinnah, the great enemy of Gandhi. Although not religious himself, Jinnah used religious themes in his speeches, calculated to inflame people and win support for his cause. Jinnah wanted a separate country—to be named Pakistan—for Muslim Indians. Violence erupted in Calcutta in August 1946, shortly after one of Jinnah's speeches. Margaret hurried to the city to photograph the terrible bloodshed.

Then she went to South India, where she visited a tannery. There she saw children from the lowest class of Hindu Indians, the untouchables, working lye into leather hides. The chemical burned their legs and arms, and repeated

Margaret's famous photograph of Gandhi, 1947

burns resulted in deformities. A short time later, Margaret went home and started writing a book about India, *Halfway to Freedom.*

The following year, on August 15, 1947, Great Britain granted independence to India and Pakistan. In the next several months, chaos reigned. Millions of people packed their belongings and rode donkeys and ox carts, or walked, from one new nation to the other in a great exodus—Hindus leaving Pakistan for India; Muslims leaving India for Pakistan. With little food, very hot weather, and illness spreading among the weak, thousands died along the way. Along the border, fighting broke out between Hindus and Muslims and a third group, the Sikhs. India was torn apart by the bloody brawls.

Muslims haul their belongings from India to the new nation of Pakistan in a great migration.

In despair over the violence, Gandhi began a fast to persuade all Indians to stop fighting. He would fast until death, if necessary. Most Indians, no matter what their religion, greatly respected Gandhi, and a fast was a particularly effective method of getting them to pay attention to his ideals. After six days, messages began pouring in to Gandhi. Peace had been restored in most areas of India, and Gandhi was so encouraged by the progress that he broke his fast.

Less than two weeks later, on the day Margaret was to leave India, she had a final interview with Gandhi in his quarters at Birla House. He asked her about her book, and he autographed a picture for her. They had a very pleasant discussion about nonviolence in the face of nuclear war, and Margaret found herself admiring Gandhi and his philosophies anew. Before she left, something stopped her. She turned back and heard herself wishing the great man good luck.

Just hours later, a member of a militant Hindu sect that believed Gandhi was too tolerant of Muslims stepped from a group of the Mahatma's followers at a public meeting and shot three bullets into his chest. Gandhi was dead.

The news shocked the world. Margaret, too, was in shock, but the photographer in her recovered. She raced to Birla House, where Gandhi's body lay on a straw mattress, surrounded by his family. She was allowed into the room, but was not to take any photographs or even to have a camera with her. But she had concealed a camera and tried to take photographs of the scene inside the room. Her flash gave her away, and several outraged Indians seized her camera, destroyed her film, and evicted her from the house.

Margaret had just as difficult a time taking photographs at Gandhi's public funeral. There were so many people at the event that she couldn't get into position to take pictures. When she finally found a spot on top of a truck, she was pulled down by the truck's occupants.

Although she was busy photographing, Margaret shared the sorrow of the crowds. She believed Gandhi's ultimate sacrifice for religious freedom and a unified India was a turning point for the new country.

Back home in Darien, Connecticut, Margaret completed *Halfway to Freedom,* in which she succeeded in explaining and analyzing the complex political situation in India. The book came out in 1949.

Margaret's next assignment for *Life* took her to South
Africa to document another extreme case of prejudice.
When Margaret arrived late in 1949, whites owned 90 per-
cent of the land and all the gold and diamond mines in South
Africa, but blacks outnumbered whites by four to one.

Margaret first arrived in Johannesburg, where she found
a system that forced black men away from their families for
18 months at a time to work in the mines. When a black man
turned 18 years old, the government levied taxes against
him—to be paid in cash rather than the livestock or grain he
was likely to have. Unless he had a receipt showing he had
paid his taxes, he was not allowed to travel outside his home.
There were few opportunities for a black man to earn money,
aside from taking a mine job, and no opportunities for him to
learn a skilled trade. Usually he had no choice but to work for
the low wages the mines paid.

Living conditions at the mines were appalling. The black
workers lived in compounds—rows of concrete houses
joined together in a settlement that was surrounded by
barbed wire. At night the workers were crowded into win-
dowless rooms to sleep. Then guards locked the compound.

Margaret also discovered that children were put to
work in vineyards and were paid partly with wine. In time,
they became addicted to alcohol and would buy even more
wine than what was given them for their work. Margaret
was horrified by what she saw, but dared not reveal her true
feelings. She knew she needed to appear impartial to be allowed access to all the things she wanted to photograph.

There were shantytowns outside the city of Johannesburg where homes were made of crates, gasoline tins, and
burlap sacks. Police frequently raided these quarters, ar-
resting men who were drunk or had committed other petty

offenses, to provide cheap prison labor for white farmers. Margaret went along on one raid and photographed frightened children peering through windows and doors as police swarmed through their grimy yards.

One Sunday Margaret saw and photographed some graceful miners in costumes, dancing tribal dances at their compound. The next day, she asked permission to go down into the gold mine with two of the dancers. At first the superintendent refused, saying their work area was too dangerous for visitors. Margaret insisted and was finally escorted far down into the mines, over a mile below the surface of the earth.

South African children participate in a protest against police raids in their compounds.

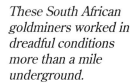

These South African goldminers worked in dreadful conditions more than a mile underground.

The temperature in this part of the mine was 100 degrees, and the air was heavy and filled with dirt. While photographing the two men, Margaret began having difficulty speaking and moving her limbs. She was moved to better air, where she quickly recovered, but she was saddened to think the men she had been photographing had to spend more than eight hours in the suffocating environment, day after day.

Margaret traveled next to the isolated and tightly guarded Diamond Coast mines. The diamond industry was controlled by one of the tightest cartels in the world. This group of exporters released a small amount of diamonds at a time in order to control the supply and keep prices high. This was done, even though rough stones that could be polished and cut for jewelry were plentiful.

During Margaret's visit, she noticed that diamond miners frequently found rough stones lying on the ground. At the end of each workday, they turned in these loose diamonds for a bonus—a sixpence (worth about 10 cents in 1950) paid in the form of a credit slip that could be used at the company store. X rays were taken of all workers as they left the mine. Armed guards and savage dogs made sure no one tried to smuggle out the diamonds.

Each night, the miners returned to their quarters. All miners, white and black, were locked in behind miles of barbed wire fencing. The white miners, however, lived with their families in a spacious area with tennis courts and playgrounds. These inequities greatly disturbed Margaret. She wasn't alone. Blacks, some South African whites, and the United Nations were bitterly opposed to the system called apartheid (apartness) in South Africa.

After seeing the harsh and dreadful life endured by the majority of people in South Africa, Margaret came home and went on lecture tours. Audiences knew Margaret was a highly paid woman who enjoyed fine clothes and a distinctive style of living. By telling them about South Africa, she made them understand why she had now come to hate gold and diamonds.

Margaret's efforts to photograph tourists waving from the Statue of Liberty nearly landed her and her helicopter pilot in trouble.

ELEVEN

The Toughest Obstacle

1951–1971

Margaret had become a legend by 1950. People told and retold stories about her; Canada named a lake near Montreal after her; and she received honorary doctorates from Rutgers University and the University of Michigan. Despite her many accomplishments, Margaret showed no signs of slowing down. She was 47 years old, her hair had turned white, and she was in excellent health. She seemed eager to tackle new challenges.

In the spring of 1951, she was the first woman to fly in the brand-new B-47 jet, an important part of the Strategic Air Command (SAC) that prepared for possible confrontation with the Soviet Union. Then Margaret took an assignment to show *Life* readers a view of America from a helicopter. She was nearly arrested for urging the pilot too close to the Statue of Liberty so she could photograph tourists waving from the monument's crown.

In September a columnist named Westbrook Pegler wrote that Margaret should never have been cleared to photograph U.S. defense secrets like the B-47. Nor should she have been allowed access to navy rescue operations that she had photographed that month, he said. Pegler noted that Margaret had been married to Erskine Caldwell, who was cited as a Communist sympathizer. Caldwell had been asked to appear before the House Committee on Un-American Activities at the request of the Federal Bureau of Investigation. Pegler also listed what he called Margaret's propaganda films of the Soviet Union in 1934, several of her photographs that reflected badly on the United States, a picture she had taken of Communist presidential candidate Earl Browder in 1936, and other examples that he interpreted as Communist leanings. Margaret was at first bewildered by the charges, then angry and determined to prove Pegler wrong.

Margaret with her camera in the cockpit of a B-47 jet. The B-47 was an important part of the U.S. post-WWII defense strategy.

She quickly proposed a plan to Ed Thompson, her editor at *Life*. She told Thompson she wanted to go to Korea, where the United States was involved in the war between North and South Korea. She would show what other photographers assigned to the war had not shown—how the fighting affected the ordinary citizens of Korea. Of course, Margaret would need to obtain accreditation from the Department of Defense before she would be cleared to travel with U.S. troops. Only a loyal American could receive such clearance. Thompson, a former senior intelligence officer, was effective in pleading her case to the Department of Defense. In the spring of 1952, Margaret was on her way to Korea.

Margaret's unique shot of the interior of a B-36 bomber that carried atomic bombs.

By the time Margaret arrived in Korea, neither the north nor the south factions were making progress into the other's territory. Discussions were under way for a peace agreement. As she began her work, Margaret hadn't decided which angle to take in her photo-essay. Then she became intrigued by the bands of Communist guerrillas that lived in the mountains of South Korea and made surprise attacks on U.N. forces behind the front. Many of these guerrillas came from South Korean villages, where Communist forces worked at converting citizens to their side. Margaret wrote about her idea:

> Sometimes when a boy had run away to join the Communists, and a neutral villager informed his mother of his whereabouts, she would climb into the mountains and implore her son to leave the Communist band. I found it deeply moving that all this conflict of beliefs was so close to home that a grieving mother would brave the perils of dark and the mountain crags to plead with her boy to come home. Here was a civil war with friend against friend, and brother against brother. Here was a war of ideas which cut through every village and through the human heart itself.

She forged into the mountains for her story. Traveling with the South Korean National Police, she was introduced to a guerrilla named Nim Churl-Jin, who had surrendered; he no longer believed in communism and wanted to go home to his family. Margaret gained permission to return him to his village, where he had a wife, a son he had never met, and a mother who thought he was dead. Margaret photographed the reunion, and her essay later ran as a lead in *Life.* With its publication, accusations about Margaret being a Communist sympathizer died away.

Margaret took this photograph of Korean guerrillas making explosives near their mountain cave, while a young member of their group keeps lookout from above.

Margaret spent her last night in Korea in a cheap hotel room, where mosquitoes bit her and rain seeped through holes in the wall. The hotel was located in a mountain village that, unknown to Margaret, was suffering an encephalitis outbreak. Mosquitoes were primary carriers of the disease. From Korea, Margaret went to Tokyo, where she danced all night with officers, forgot to eat, and got a chill. She spent the next two days sleeping on airline flights, missing meals and plane connections, to get back to the United States. Once back in New York, she behaved erratically. *Life* editors assumed she had battle fatigue.

Generally, Margaret was strong and healthy. She often missed meals, slept anywhere, worked long hours in bad weather, yet never became ill. She was called Maggie the Indestructible. This time, however, she began to experience strange aches and weaknesses, primarily on the left side of her body. She had difficulty climbing stairs and sometimes staggered when she walked. She didn't know why.

Margaret was well enough to go on a successful lecture tour, and she continued working for *Life*. Her health problems persisted, however, and she visited specialist after specialist to pinpoint the cause of her symptoms.

Finally, in January of 1954, Margaret saw Dr. Howard Rusk, who diagnosed her condition as Parkinson's disease. Unlike many people who have Parkinson's disease, Margaret seldom experienced its most obvious symptom— uncontrollable shaking. Dr. Rusk told her that in her case, the disease would progressively stiffen her limbs and rob her of her sense of balance. Simple tasks would become increasingly difficult. Dr. Rusk put her on a strict exercise program to slow the stiffening, and she followed it faithfully.

Margaret traced her disease back to the mosquito-filled

room during the encephalitis epidemic in Korea. She never regretted having gone there, however. She simply said, "If I had . . . to make a choice between getting my photos in the fog, rain, and wild mountains of Korea set against the risks involved, I would still choose to get my story—Parkinson's or no Parkinson's."

Margaret tried to hide her illness, but many of her colleagues knew something was wrong. The public didn't catch on, because Margaret's work still appeared prominently. She still took pictures for *Life,* and her photographs were included in shows, most notably the prestigious Family of Man exhibit that opened at New York's Museum of Modern Art in 1955 and was eventually displayed in over 30 countries.

That same year, Margaret asked Henry Luce at *Life* for the assignment to the moon, if and when a photographer was assigned to go on a space mission, and he agreed to give it to her. She was sure she would recover from her illness and go on that assignment.

Margaret continued working, but her skills were eroding quickly. Reporters had to load film into her camera for her. *Life* continued to give her assignments, but after 1957, she could no longer handle them. She continued lecturing until 1958. Then Margaret went public with her illness. In June 1959, *Life* ran a story about Margaret's fight against the effects of Parkinson's disease—illustrated with photographs taken by Alfred Eisenstaedt, a close friend of Margaret's. By then Margaret had undergone brain surgery to reverse some of her symptoms. In 1960 "The Margaret Bourke-White Story" was shown on national television. Margaret had been present at the filming. In 1961 she had a second operation, this time to reverse symptoms on the right side of her body. The disease had spread.

*One of Alfred
Eisenstaedt's photos
shows Margaret
crumbling the pages
of a newspaper into
balls. The activity was
a form of physical
therapy to keep her
hands and wrists from
stiffening.*

To protect her privacy, Margaret burned many of her diaries, but in 1963, she published an autobiography entitled *Portrait of Myself.* It is a modest and interesting, if not totally accurate, account of her life.

As the years went on, Margaret's condition worsened. By 1969 she couldn't walk without assistance—a housekeeper and a physical therapist or companion helped her at home. Even as the disease progressed, when she could dance better than she could walk, Margaret enjoyed evenings out with men. Still, she was alone much of the time. During her last years, she worked on a second autobiography by dictating it slowly; her speech had been affected by the second operation.

In January 1971, an exhibit of Margaret's work opened at the Witkin Gallery in New York, and Margaret was there for the celebration. In June, she attended Plainfield High School's 50-year reunion. She visited with former classmates from a wheelchair, although she could manage no more than a whisper. At home later that summer, she fell and broke several ribs. She was confined to a hospital bed, unable to do the exercises that had been so effective at slowing the disease. She died on August 27, 1971, at the age of 67.

Margaret was fortunate to have lived and worked in an age when still photography evolved as the primary means of showing news to people. For a while, until television became available to many people, news photographers had no competition. Photographs gave meaning, identification, and real proof to stories. *Life* used this medium better than any other publication at the time, and Margaret was one of the magazine's best photographers. She helped Americans understand the biggest news events of the day.

Margaret had managed to become a successful photographer before *Fortune* and *Life* even existed. Even so, these influential magazines were as important to her growth and development as her work was to their popularity and success. They gave her fame, wealth, adventure, and social awareness. She gave back her legacy, a body of work that makes her one of the great visual artists of all time.

Sources

p.8   Margaret Bourke-White, *Portrait of Myself* (New York: Simon and Schuster, 1963), 78.

p.8   *American Magazine,* (November 1930), 66.

p.9   Iris Noble, *Cameras and Courage* (New York: Julian Messner, 1973), 7–8.

p.9   "The Best Advice I Ever Had," *Reader's Digest* (May 1957), 84–86.

p.11   Bourke-White, *Portrait of Myself,* 14.

p.15   Ibid., 18.

p.21   Goldberg, *Margaret Bourke-White: A Biography* (New York: Harper and Row, 1986), 28.

p.27   Bourke-White, *Portrait of Myself,* 27.

p.29   Ibid., 28.

p.31   Ibid., 32.

p.31   Ibid., 32.

p.36   Goldberg, *Margaret Bourke-White,* 72.

p.40   Ibid., 77.

p.41   Bourke-White, *Portrait of Myself,* 52.

p.45   Ibid., 60

p.47   Goldberg, *Margaret Bourke-White,* 91.

p.47   Ibid., 101.

p.48   Bourke-White, *Portrait of Myself,* 64.

p.49   Goldberg, *Margaret Bourke-White,* 105.

p.49   Bourke-White, *Portrait of Myself,* 191.

p.55   Goldberg, *Margaret Bourke-White,* 98.

p.57   Ibid., 126.

p.60   Margaret Bourke-White, *Eyes on Russia* (New York: Simon and Schuster, 1931), 65.

p.60   Ibid., dedication.

p.62   *Fortune,* (January 1933), 57.

p.63   *Time,* (December 14, 1931), 56.

p.67   Bourke-White, *Portrait of Myself,* 106.

p.79   Goldberg, *Margaret Bourke-White,* 218.

p.82   *U.S. Camera,* (May 1940), 43.

p.83   Goldberg, *Margaret Bourke-White,* 229.

p.88   Margaret Bourke-White, *Shooting the Russian War* (New York: Simon and Schuster, 1942), 217.

p.88   Goldberg, *Margaret Bourke-White,* 248.

p.92   Bourke-White, *Portrait of Myself,* 203.

p.94   Ibid., 308.

p.97   Ibid., 310.

p.97   Ibid., 258–259.

p.114 Ibid., 332.

p.117 Sean Callahan, *The Photographs of Margaret Bourke-White* (Greenwich, Connecticut: New York Graphic Society, 1972), 177.

Selected Bibliography

Writings of Margaret Bourke-White

Dear Fatherland, Rest Quietly. New York: Simon and Schuster, 1946.

Eyes on Russia. New York: Simon and Schuster, 1931.

Halfway to Freedom. New York: Simon and Schuster, 1949.

North of the Danube. New York: Duell, Sloan and Pearce, 1939. With Erskine Caldwell.

Portrait of Myself. New York: Simon and Schuster, 1963.

A Report on the American Jesuits. New York: Farrar, Straus, and Cudahy, 1956. With John LaFarge.

Say, Is This the U.S.A.? New York: Duell, Sloan and Pearce, 1941. With Erskine Caldwell.

Shooting the Russian War. New York: Simon and Schuster, 1942.

They Called It Purple Heart Valley. New York: Simon and Schuster, 1944.

You Have Seen Their Faces. New York: Viking Press, 1937. With Erskine Caldwell.

Other Sources

Block, M., ed., "Margaret Bourke-White," *Current Biography.* New York, 1940, pp. 862–863.

Brown, Theodore M. *Margaret Bourke-White: Photojournalist.* Ithaca, New York: Andrew Dickson White Museum of Art, Cornell University, 1972.

Caldwell, Erskine. *With All My Might.* Atlanta, Georgia: Peachtree Press, 1987.

Callahan, Sean, ed., *The Photographs of Margaret Bourke-White.* Greenwich, Connecticut: New York Graphic Society, 1972.

Fortune. Issues published during the years 1930 through 1933.

Goldberg, Vicki. *Margaret Bourke-White: A Biography.* New York: Harper and Row, 1986.

Himber, Charlotte. *Famous in their Twenties.* New York: Association Press, 1942.

Life. Issues published during the years 1936 through 1971.

Siegel, Beatrice. *An Eye on the World.* New York: Frederick Warne, 1980.

Silverman, Jonathan. *For the World to See: The Life of Margaret Bourke-White.* New York: Viking Press, 1983.

Stott, William. *Documentary Expression and Thirties America.* New York: Oxford University Press, 1973.

Tucker, Anne, ed., *The Woman's Eye.* New York: Alfred A. Knopf, 1976.

Index

Africa, 92, 94–95, 106–109
Arctic Circle, 74–75
Atkinson, J. Hampton, 94

B-17s, 91–92, 94
Bemis, Alfred Hall (Beme),
  37–38, 41, 43, 45
Bolwell, Charlie, 43
Bourke-White, Margaret
  on assignments, 49, 57, 65,
    68–75, 81–89, 91–99,
    101–109, 111, 117
  author, 23–24, 59, 61, 81, 89,
    97, 99, 103, 105, 118 (see
    also individual titles)

Bourke-White, Margaret (cont'd)
  awards for photography, 47
  birth, 8
  childhood, 9–15
  coping with and overcoming
    fears, 9, 24–25
  death, 118
  divorce from Erskine
    Caldwell, 89
  divorce from Everett
    Chapman, 46
  education, 17–23, 28–29
  exhibits of photography, 57,
    63, 74, 117–118
  films by, 61–62
  health problems, 24, 82,
    116–118
  influences on Margaret's
    photography, 19, 38, 70
  machinery, early interest in,
    15
  marriage to Erskine
    Caldwell, 79, 81–86, 88–89
  marriage to Everett
    Chapman, 25, 27–29
  military career, 89–99,
    113–116
  nature, love of, 9–12, 14, 20,
    23, 83
  pets, 10–11, 23, 59, 81
  photography, early interest
    in, 15
  photojournalism, pioneer in
    field of, 51, 73
  pilot, 65, 111
  scientist, ambitions to
    become a, 10–11, 23
  social life, 18, 23, 29, 51, 55,
    118
  style of, 23, 33, 35, 38–39, 63,
    75
  teacher and lecturer, 20–21,
    28, 59, 63, 74, 89, 95, 109,
    117

Margaret, age 11

122

Bourke-White, Margaret (cont'd)
    teenager, 17–23
    See also photography by
        Margaret Bourke-White
Bourke-White Photography
    Studio, 32–33

Caldwell, Erskine (Margaret's
    second husband), 67–70,
    73–76, 78–79, 81–86, 88–89,
    112
Camp Agaming, 20–21
Canada, 18–19, 74, 111
Chapman, Everett (Chappie,
    Margaret's first husband),
    23–25, 27–29, 46–47
Chapman, Mrs. (Everett's
    mother), 27–29
Chrysler Building, 7–8, 59, 63
Churchill, Winston, 91
Churl-Jin, Nim, 114
Cleveland, 28, 31, 33, 46–48, 55
Cleveland Chamber of
    Commerce, 38
Columbia University, 19, 67
communism, 112, 114–115
Cornell University, 29–31, 47
Czechoslovakia, 76, 78–79

Dear Fatherland, Rest Quietly, 99
Doolittle, General Jimmy, 94

Eisenstaedt, Alfred, 117
England, 81, 91
Eyes on Russia, 59

Fortune magazine, 48–51, 53,
    56–57, 59, 62

Gandhi, Mahatma Mohandas,
    101–105
Georgia, 62
Germany, 57, 62, 76, 78–79,
    81–83, 85, 89, 97–98

Graubner, Oscar, 7–8, 72
Great Britain, 81, 101
Great Depression, 51–53, 63

Hague, Frank, 76
Halfway to Freedom, 103, 105
Hall Printing Press Company, 14
Head, Henry R., 30
Hicks, Wilson, 83, 85, 88
Hitler, Adolf, 76, 78, 81, 98
Hopkins, Harry, 87

India, 100–105
Ingersoll, Ralph, 82
Italy, 89, 95–97, 99

Jackson, H. F. (Jack), 41, 43
Jacobson, Madge, 21
Jews, 24–25, 79, 98
    discrimination against, 24,
        79, 98
Jinnah, Mohammed Ali, 102

Korea, 113–117
Kulas, Elroy, 40–41, 45

Leiter, Earl, 41, 45
Life magazine, 66, 68–79, 81–85,
    87, 89, 93, 95, 101, 106, 111,
    114, 116–119
Lloyd-Smith, Parker, 48–51
Luce, Henry R., 47–48, 72, 117
Luf, Tubby, 17

Moscow, Russia, 58–59, 85–88
Moskowitz, Benjamin, 31
Munger, Jessie, 21

New York, 8, 19, 29–30, 48, 57,
    59, 70, 116, 118
North of the Blue Danube, 78

Otis Steel mill, 39–43, 47–49

Food line in Louisville, Kentucky, 1937

Pakistan, 102–104
Papurt, Jerry, 96–97
Parkinson's disease, 116–117
Patton, General George S., 97
Pegler, Westbrook, 111–112
Phillips, John, 78
photography by Margaret
  Bourke-White
    advertising and commercial,
      38, 39–40, 46, 51, 56, 59,
      63–65
    architectural, 32, 35–36, 39,
      46, 52–53
    aviation, 65, 67, 90–91,
      94–95, 111–113
    in college magazines, 23, 29
    industrial, 34, 38, 40–43,
      44–46, 47–51, 57–59, 72–73

photography by Margaret
  Bourke-White, (cont'd)
    in national magazines and
      newspapers, 35, 45–46, 47,
      56, 74 *(see also Fortune*
      magazine; *Life* magazine;
      PM newspaper; *Time*
      magazine)
    landscape, 36, 39–40, 46
    nature, 74, 83–84
    people, 56, 69–71, 73, 76–77,
      84, 88, 91, 102–103,
      106–109
    postcards, 21, 29–30
    risks in obtaining photos,
      7–8, 20, 41, 52–53, 65,
      86–87, 93, 94
    war, 84–99, 114–115

Plainfield High School, 17, 118
PM newspaper, 82–84
Portrait of Myself, 118

Rusk, Dr. Howard, 116
Russia, 57, 60–61. *See also*
    Moscow, Russia
Rutgers University, 19, 111
Ruthven, Alexander G., 23

Sargent, Peggy, 72, 79
Say, Is This the U.S.A.?, 84
Selassie, Haile, 91
Shooting the Russian War, 89
South Africa, 106–109
Soviet Union, 57, 61, 63, 85,
    87–88, 111, 112. *See also*
    Georgia; Russia
Stalin, Joseph, 57, 87–88
Story of Steel, The, 45

Terminal Tower, 32, 40, 46, 55
They Call It Purple Heart Valley,
    97

Thompson, Ed, 113
Time magazine, 47–48, 68. *See
    also Fortune* magazine; *Life*
    magazine
Trade Winds, 38
Turkey, 82

University of Michigan, 22–23,
    111

White, Clarence H., 19, 47
White, Joseph (Margaret's
    father), 8–10, 14–15, 18–19, 24
White, Minnie (Margaret's
    mother), 8–9, 12–13, 20, 24, 31,
    67
White, Roger (Margaret's
    brother), 9–10, 16, 18, 31
White, Ruth (Margaret's sister),
    9–10, 13–14, 16, 18
World War II, 81–99

You Have Seen Their Faces, 71,
    73–74, 81

Photo Acknowledgments

Photographs in this book are reproduced by permission of:
the National Archives, pp. 2 (208-PU-2215-3), 26 (66-M-43-1), 32 (66-M 43-3), 58 (131-WP-91-1), 80 (208-PU-221-S-1), and 127 (131-WP-91-3); the Estate of Margaret Bourke-White, pp. 6 (by Oscar Graubner), 11, 12, 13, 14, 16, 19, 20, 22, 25, 30, 33, 34, 37, 39 (by Earl Leiter), 40 (both), 42, 44, 46, 50, 52, 54, 56, 60, 61, 64, 66, 71 (both), 74, 77, 78, 84, 85, 92, 96, and 122; and Margaret Bourke-White, *Life* magazine, © Time Inc., 72, 87, 88, 90, 98, 99, 100, 103, 104, 107, 108, 110, 112, 113, 115, 118 (by Alfred Eisenstaedt), and 124.

Front cover photograph is reproduced by permission of the Estate of Margaret Bourke-White. The back cover photograph is reproduced courtesy of the National Archives (111-SC-182029).

Publisher's Note

The placement of a black edge around Margaret Bourke-White's photographs throughout this book is a graphic design element. Lerner Publications Company has reproduced the photographs exactly as provided by the Margaret Bourke-White Collection at Syracuse University or the National Archives, except for slight cropping occasionally needed to accommodate the text design.

Margaret Bourke-White's photograph of Novodevichy Monastery in Moscow, 1930

About the Author

Emily Keller is an English teacher who has published many poems and magazine and newspaper articles. She has long wanted to write a biography of the type of woman she admired as a child—one who was independent, adventurous, and successful. *Margaret Bourke-White* is her first book. Ms. Keller lives on Cayuga Island in Niagara Falls, New York, and has two daughters and three grandsons.